THOMAS COLE

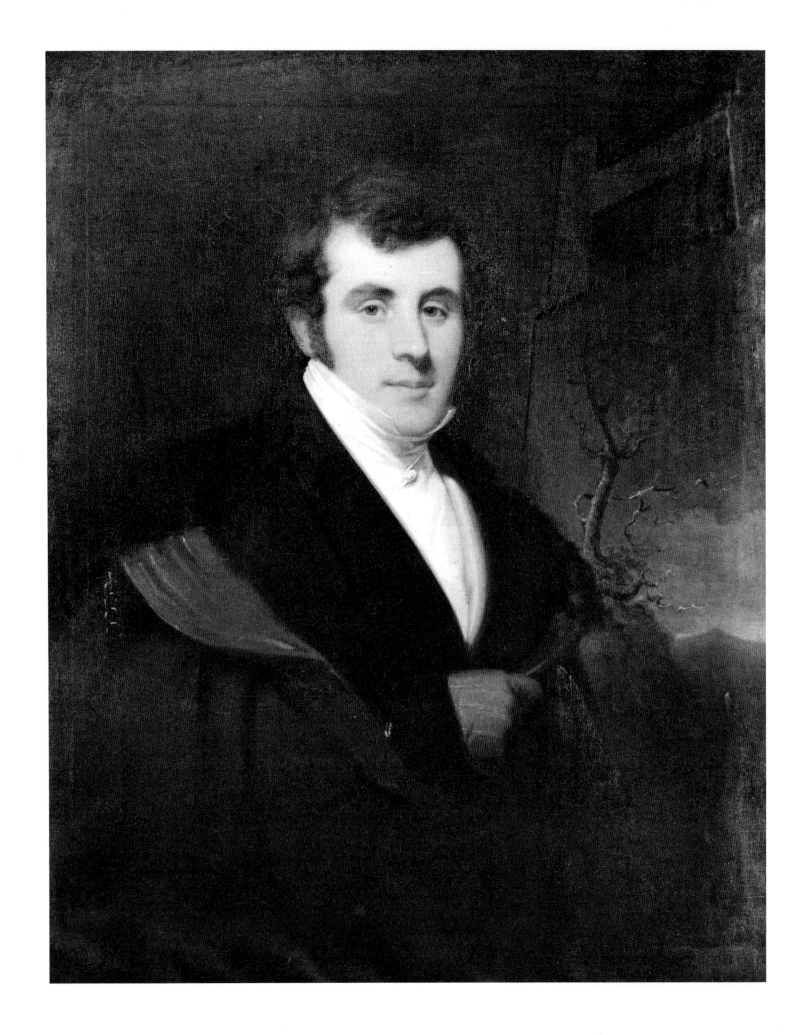

THOMAS COLE

by Matthew Baigell

WATSON-GUPTILL PUBLICATIONS/NEW YORK

Frontispiece

PORTRAIT OF THOMAS COLE
by Thomas Seir Cummings.
Oil on canvas, 36¼″ x 29¼″ (92 x 74.3 cm).
Albany Institute of History and Art,
Albany, New York.

First published 1981 in New York by Watson-Guptill Publications,
a division of Billboard Publications, Inc.,
1515 Broadway, New York, N.Y. 10036

Library of Congress Cataloging in Publication Data

Baigell, Matthew.
    Thomas Cole.

    Bibliography: p.
    Includes index.
    1. Cole, Thomas, 1801–1848. 2. Landscape painters—
United States—Biography. I. Title.
ND237.C6B3   759.13   81–3379
ISBN 0-8230-0647-6   AACR2

Manufactured in Japan

First Printing, 1981

For Renee,
with whom I've traveled these
and other woods

I jumped at the opportunity to write this book, which concentrates on Thomas Cole's landscapes, because I have often camped with my family in those parts of the Northeast with which Cole is most closely identified—the Catskill Highlands, the Adirondacks and the White Mountains, and the coast of Maine. In addition to having an excuse to revisit several sites the artist painted, I was also provided with the opportunity to review the extensive published and unpublished literature on Cole and on the period from 1825 to 1850 in which he flourished. Of greatest help were the several dissertations written on aspects of Cole's art as well as the microfilms and photostatic copies of his writings on deposit at the Archives of American Art and the New-York Historical Society.

I especially want to thank Renee Baigell, Howard Green, and Dr. Allen Kaufman for sharing with me their knowledge of nineteenth-century American literature and history; and Dr. Doris Sommer and Renee Baigell for providing interpretative information for Plates 7 and 30. I also want to thank the Watson-Guptill staff who have contributed their efforts to this book: Dorothy Spencer, Senior Editor; Betty Vera, Associate Editor; Barbara Wood, who copy-edited the text; Bob Fillie, who designed the book; and Ellen Greene, graphic production.

The chronology is derived primarily from the Ph.D. dissertations of Kenneth James LaBudde ("The Mind of Thomas Cole," 1954) and Elwood C. Parry III ("Thomas Cole's 'The Course of Empire': A Study in Serial Imagery," 1970).

1801 Is born on February 1, in Bolton-le-Moor, Lancashire, England, the seventh child of Mary and James Cole, a woolen manufacturer.

1810 Goes to school in Chester.

ca. 1815 Is apprenticed to an engraver of designs in a calico print factory.

ca. 1817 Works as an engraver's assistant in Liverpool.

1818 Cole family arrives in Philadelphia on July 3. Thomas remains while rest of family moves to Steubenville, Ohio, and works as a textile print designer and an engraver of illustrations for John Bunyan's *Holy War*.

1819 Sails for St. Eustatius, West Indies, on January 4. In summer, joins family in Steubenville and aids father in wallpaper-manufacturing enterprise.

1820 Advertises as art teacher in January. Meets itinerant artist named Stein, from whom he learns fundamentals of painting.

1821 Paints portraits and landscapes.

1822 Tours Ohio from February to August in search of commissions. Does religious paintings and paints scenery for Thespian Society during winter of 1822–23.

1823 In spring, joins family which had previously moved to Pittsburgh. Begins to sketch out-of-doors. Leaves for Philadelphia in November. Draws at Pennsylvania Academy of the Fine Arts and makes ornamental figures. Works for a japanner. Exhibits a landscape at academy in 1824.

1825 Moves to New York City in spring. Travels up Hudson River Valley in summer and sells three landscapes, to John Trumbull, William Dunlap, and Asher B. Durand. Meets early patrons George W. Bruen and George Featherstonaugh. Short story "Emma Morton" appears in *Saturday Evening Post* (May 25).

1826 Spends winter in upper Hudson region and summer in Catskill, the village that becomes his summer residence until he moves there permanently in 1836. Is elected to and exhibits in National Academy of Design. Also exhibits at American Academy of Fine Arts. Shows works at former throughout his life and at latter at least until 1828. Robert Gilmor, Jr., becomes important patron.

1827 First tours of White Mountains in October.

1829 Travels to Niagara Falls in May. Sails for England on June 1. Meets Sir Thomas Laurence, John Constable, and John M. W. Turner there.

1830 Exhibits at British Institution and Royal Academy (in 1831 also).

1831 Starts tour of Continent on May 4. Visits Louvre and architectural monuments in Paris. Arrives in Florence in June.

1832 Visits Rome in winter and, in early spring, travels to Naples and Paestum. Makes first study for a panorama—sketch of Bay of Naples. Returns to Florence and then departs for New York, arriving in November.

1833 Meets Luman Reed, an important patron for whom he proposes series that becomes *The Course of Empire*. (Had developed the idea as early as 1827.)

1835 Writes "Lecture on American Scenery," which is published the following year as "Essay on American Scenery." (See bibliography.)

1836 Marries Maria Bartow and settles in Catskill. Completes *The Course of Empire*.

1837 Paints *Departure* and *Return*, second set of his paintings in series.

1838 Completes *Past* and *Present*. Enters architectural competition for Ohio State Capitol and wins third prize.

1839 Begins *Voyage of Life*, completed the following year. Tours White Mountains in July and western New York in August.

1841 Is in London from August to September, then travels through France and Switzerland before arriving in Rome in November. Paints second version of *Voyage of Life*, completed in 1842.

1842 Visits Sicily in April. Returns to London in June and arrives in New York on July 30. Joins Episcopal Church.

1843 Lectures on Sicilian scenery and publishes two articles on Sicilian scenery and antiquities. (See bibliography.)

1844 Accepts Frederick Church as pupil. Visits Mount Desert, Maine, in August. Projects several paintings in series, virtually all with religious content, including *Sowing and Reaping*; *Life, Death, and Immortality*; and *L'Allegro* and *Il Penseroso*. Of these, only the last is completed (1845).

1845 Plans *The Cross and the World*, which remains unfinished at death.

1847 Visits Niagara Falls in August.

1848 Dies on February 8. William Cullen Bryant's funeral oration delivered at National Academy of Design on May 4. During same month a retrospective exhibition is held at American Art-Union.

THOMAS COLE

THOMAS COLE is one of those marvelous nineteenth-century figures like Ralph Waldo Emerson whose works warrant continued scrutiny and provoke endless speculation. Cole can be approached by considering several aspects of his career: he was a conveyor of European culture to America, a developer of America's own growing cultural heritage, a thematic innovator, a bridge between generations, and a subject for countless studies relating his thought and art to a variety of intellectual, religious, and social trends of the time. He can also be compared to earlier artists of the colonies and young republic who without formal training decided at a youthful age to explore the range of subject matter lying beyond the artistic staple of those years, portraiture.

To that end, Cole had already decided by 1825, when he left Philadelphia for New York City, to concentrate on landscape and religious themes (see the chronology for biographical information). The distinction between these two categories was not necessarily as clear in Cole's mind as one might imagine, since in his poems, which he wrote throughout his life, and in his published and unpublished essays, he often alluded to the apprehension of God through observation of nature. For instance, in the early poem "The Wild," written about 1826, Cole wrote:

Friends of my heart, lovers of nature's works,
Let me transport you to those wild, blue mountains
That rear their summits near the Hudson's wave;
Though not the loftiest that begirt the land,
They yet sublimely rise, on their heights
Your soul may have a sweet foretaste of heaven. . . .[1]

In fact, the two themes, religion and the landscape, were inextricably combined in his work, and these, in turn, were linked to his understanding of the function of art. Cole believed "the subject [of art] should be pure and lofty . . . , an impressive lesson must be taught, an important scene illustrated—a moral, religious or poetic effect be produced on the mind," and that "chiaroscuro, color, form should always be subservient to the subject, and never be raised to the dignity of an end."[2] Clearly, he was opposed to the point of view, best represented by Edgar Allan Poe in

the first half of the century, that technique, or the means of art, should be considered more important than its message. Cole, in his belief that art ought to be a ladder by which people might rise to see spiritual reality shining above base nature, followed an old and still honored Anglo-American tradition, dating back at least to Sir Philip Sidney's *Apologie for Poetrie*, written in the 1580s, of using art as a means of moral instruction. Given the conservative tendencies of America's cultural arbiters of the time, it was difficult to think otherwise, and Cole was no rebel.[3]

His art, however, did coincide with two new currents of thought that were permeating American society and by 1820 had gained considerable force: first, the nationalistic interest in American scenery, and second, the religious awe with which the scenery was increasingly examined. To simplify brutally, the American landscape, no longer the howling wilderness of the Puritans, was considered the prime symbol of the American nation as well as a revelation of God's handiwork. Nature, competing with the Bible as a source of religious inspiration, became confused in the eyes of many with scriptural revelation. It was considered, in some measure, extended genesis.[4] The wilderness revealed the work and hand of God, and the domestication of the landscape represented the American people working out God's plan on the continent. This mixture of nationalism and religion led to the paradoxical praise both of the wilderness and of its destruction by the advance of American civilization. Cole's importance lies in the fact that after 1825, the year in which his paintings became well known, those tendencies could be read more profoundly in his works than in the paintings of any other artist in the country.

Cole was fortunate to have settled in Philadelphia in 1824 and then in New York City the following year because landscape artists, writers, and publishers in both communities were helping to establish a favorable climate of opinion as well as a stylistic base from which an imaginative, aggressive, and determined artist like Cole could spring. Most of the artists were English and favored the topographical manner of painting then common in England. A typical work included detailed studies of relatively small-scale vistas and of buildings with their surrounding grounds. For the most part, artists avoided the styles of Claude Lorrain and Salvator Rosa, whose works were considered models for landscapists in the eighteenth and early nineteenth centuries. The former's paintings were characterized by softly rolling landscapes and gradual spatial recessions, often populated by mythological

figures. Rosa's works were, in contrast, filled with jagged elements, and his themes were usually more emotional and bombastic. In the language of the day, Lorrain's work was considered beautiful, whereas Rosa's was sublime.

Artists whom Cole might have met, or whose works he probably knew, included, in Philadelphia, William and Thomas Birch, who had arrived in 1794; William Goombridge, who had also come about that time; John Hill, who had come in 1816; and Joshua Shaw, around 1817. Charles Willson Peale, who lived in Philadelphia, had worked in the topographical manner as early as 1801, and Philadelphia-born Thomas Doughty began painting landscapes in that city before 1820. New York had attracted Archibald and Alexander Robertson in the 1790s, William Winstanley in 1790, William Guy Wall in 1818, and William Bennett in 1826. After settling in New York in 1825, Cole probably saw the landscapes of John Trumbull and John Vanderlyn, two Americans who painted in the grand manner.

PERHAPS THE TWO most important works reflecting the new interest in landscape, which Cole would have known, were *Picturesque Views of American Scenery* (Philadelphia, 1819–21), the first American publication with large, colored landscape illustrations, and *Hudson River Portfolio* (New York, 1821–25). The former contained twenty aquatints by John Hill of watercolors by Joshua Shaw, and the latter included twenty engravings by Hill after William Guy Wall's paintings.

When in Philadelphia, Cole might have met the English émigré John Haviland, who had arrived in 1816 and was perhaps the most knowledgeable architect in the country at the time. His *Builder's Assistant* contained passages on theories of the Picturesque as well as on the relationship of trees to their sites, speculations that may have influenced Cole's thoughts on such matters.[5] Of less immediate consequence for Cole was the policy of the Philadelphia magazines *Portfolio* and *Atkinson's Casket* to publish regularly illustrations of American scenery (as early as 1809 in the *Portfolio*). Both magazines often included detailed essays on particular landscape sites.

Several authors, of course, also helped fuel the rising interest in wild and rural nature as well as

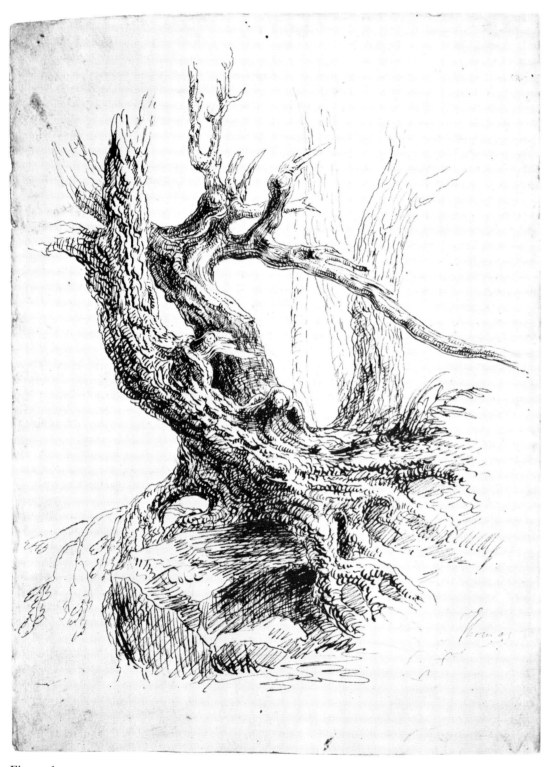

Figure 1

GNARLED TREE TRUNK
Ink on paper,
14 13/16" x 10 11/16" (37.5 x 27 cm).
Courtesy of The Detroit Institute of Arts,
William H. Murphy Fund.

its associations with nationalism and religion. These included Michel Guillaume Jean de Crèvecoeur (*Letters from an American Farmer*, 1782), Thomas Jefferson (*Notes on the State of Virginia*, 1785), William Bartram (*Travels Through North and South Carolina, Georgia, East and West Florida*, 1792), and Alexander Wilson (*The Foresters: Description of a Pedestrian Tour of the Fall of the Niagara in the Autumn of 1804*, 1804). Soon after Cole arrived in New York City, he became acquainted with such Knickerbocker figures as poet William Cullen Bryant and novelist James Fenimore Cooper, whose broad interests in the landscape have often been compared to those of Cole (some of which will be indicated in what follows).[6]

Cole, because of his personal tastes and artistic intelligence, became the leader of the rising school of landscape painters not long after he settled in New York City. By 1829, when he visited Europe for the first time, he was acknowledged to be the major American landscapist. During the preceding four years, he painted landscapes in the topographical mode and in a manner that combined aspects of Claude Lorrain's and Salvator Rosa's styles. Although he would later insist that he was not a mere "leaf painter," he completed landscape paintings that seem to have little meaning beyond the handsome views contained within them, as well as other works freighted with religious and literary meaning. In general, as in Fenimore Cooper's novels of the 1820s and 1830s, such as *The Pioneers*, landscape features in Cole's paintings of this time clearly dominate thematic elements. (The reverse occurs in both Cooper's and Cole's late works.) Regardless of theme or style, however, Cole's works are unique in American art because for the first time the viewer appears to be catapulted directly into the American wilderness. Never before had an American artist captured so completely the look and feel of raw nature as well as the apparent total indifference of nature to man's presence or intentions. These early landscapes simultaneously communicate feelings of wonder and fear.

Cole painted the scruffy underbrush, broken tree stumps (symbolic of life cycles in nature), jagged mountain profiles, and unkempt mountainsides in great detail, generally raising the viewpoint several feet above ground. From this slightly elevated perch he portrayed the wilderness as if seen for the first time. Small figures placed on rocks or lookouts contrast with the vast and magnificent areas encompassed within these paintings. However much the viewer wants to find in them evidence of and insight into God's hand in the affairs of the world or America's unique status among the world's nations, the

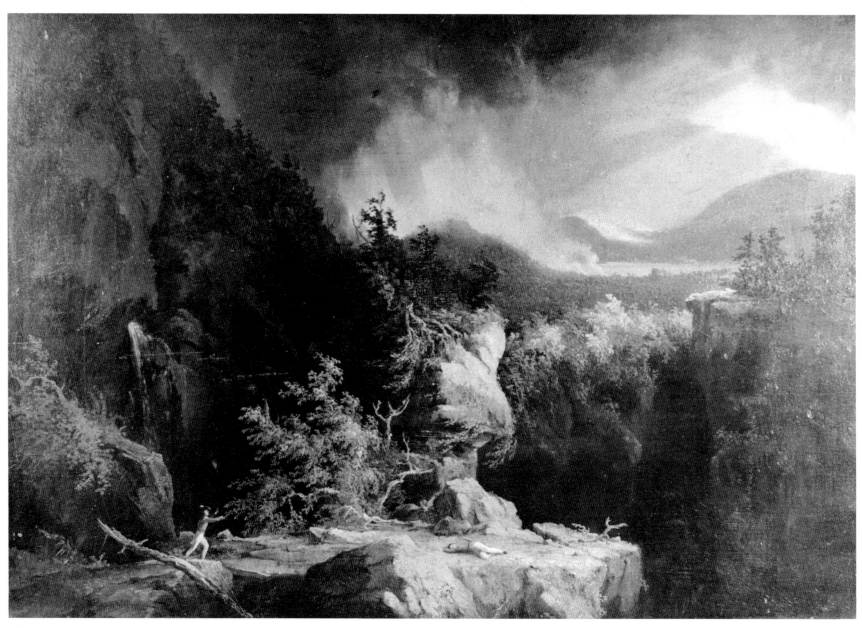

Figure 2

GELYNA
1826. 24″ x 34½″ (61 x 87.6 cm).
Courtesy of the Fort Ticonderoga Museum,
Ticonderoga, New York.

paintings also recall both the pleasures and fears of wandering through the pathless wilderness. (The possibility of a bear or wolf sniffing around one's camp at night was enough to scare anybody witless; hence the apparent paradox when contemporary authors of travel and nature books gloried in scenes of raw wilderness but were relieved by signs of habitation and settlement.)

Despite Cole's seemingly ingenuous style, his early works are actually composed very tightly. In virtually every one (and throughout his career) he imposed two long, broken diagonals forming a large X across mountain slopes, trees, and giant boulders. A diagonal might skim a hill's profile in the middle distance or course along the edges of a darkened area, but its trajectory is often seen clearly. This structural device adds emotional wallop, especially in the early works, because it invariably overwhelms the few foreground horizontals. These do not have the visual strength to suggest repose or an easy and casual entry into the picture space. The viewer, as if standing on the brink of a precipice, cannot look at the foreground as an extension of his own space because it is often omitted. In addition, Cole arbitrarily varied sunlit and shaded areas, thus providing hillsides and steep inclines with extreme topographical variation as well as suggestions of mystery and even terror. Despite boundless detail, not all parts of a painting are clear and easy to read, and it appears as if abrupt drops into endless space lurk in the uneven terrain behind rock outcroppings or clumps of trees.

THESE PAINTINGS mirror an odd union of refinement of feeling, based on artistic tradition and authority, with a relish of painting wild nature as experienced individually. In works such as *Kaaterskill Falls* (Plate 2), the tensions between these opposite formal attractions compete to a degree then unprecedented in American art, especially in the imposition of crossed diagonals for compositional purposes on the singular vantage point of the artist. Behind this solution, or compromise, lay the problems Cole faced as the knowledgeable heir of enduring values in Anglo-American culture and as the keen observer of a landscape for which compositional recipes had not yet been invented or a theoretical framework developed to visualize nationalistic beliefs. Cole might have asked himself: What was the American equivalent of an English landscape painting or of views of the Italian countryside which contained houses, manicured shrubbery, peasants, mythological figures, or ancient architectural remains? Perhaps he was fortunate never to have seen, as late as 1827, a good European landscape painting, since he was then able to create works that despite the influence of European thought were still tied directly to the American landscape.

In the previous year, 1826, Cole had expressed his artistic procedures and concerns to an early patron, Robert Gilmor, Jr., in a celebrated interchange of letters.[7] Cole, of course, drew on the entire history of academic and neoclassical thought, but we need go no further back than to Sir Joshua Reynolds's *Discourses on Art*, delivered from 1769 to 1790 when he was president of the Royal Academy, to locate the sources of Cole's aesthetic beliefs. Believing that the study of nature was important, Cole nevertheless opposed the mere imitation of nature (Discourses 6, 7, 10, 12, and 13). At the same time, Cole also rejected art derived entirely from the imagination of the artist (Discourses 6 and 9). Instead, he wanted to invent compositions based on imaginative interpretations of nature. Perhaps the ideal painting was one in which, as Cole explained to Gilmor, "the most lovely and perfect parts of Nature may be brought together, and combined in a whole that shall surpass in beauty and effect any picture painted from a single view"(Discourses 3 and 13).

Cole also sought the general form of an object rather than its particular shape, even though he often made incredibly detailed sketches on the site. On at least two occasions he described his intentions clearly. In a letter to Gilmor, written in May 1835, Cole said that he preferred to have the various landscape forms—trees, rocks, and so on— "as strongly impressed on my mind as possible and by looking intently on an object for twenty minutes I can go to my room and paint it with much more truth than I could if I employed several hours on the spot."[8] He believed that in this way he would become "more intimately acquainted with the characteristic of the spirit of Nature" and "what Nature is and painting ought to be." And to fellow artist Asher B. Durand he wrote on January 4, 1838, "Have you not found?—I have—that I never succeed in painting scenes, however beautiful, immediately on returning from them. I must wait for time to draw a veil over the common details, the unessential parts, which shall leave the great features, whether the beautiful or the sublime, dominant in the mind."[9] But this method, too, was probably derived from Reynolds, who in Discourse 11 reminded the landscape painter to show general effects rather than particulars.

Even if Cole had not read Reynolds (which is inconceivable), he might have come upon these ideas in Archibald Alison's book, *Essays on the Nature and Principles of Taste*, first published in 1790, which Cole knew at least by 1829. (His friend William Cullen Bryant was familiar with it as early as 1810.)[10] For example, Alison suggested that artists who are overly concerned with detail suppress their imaginations and impair their sense of beauty. The emotion of beauty, he maintained, can be reawakened "by relaxing this vigor of attention, and resigning ourselves again to the natural stream of our thoughts." He also thought that a landscapist, in order to give unity to a composition, needs to stress his sense of invention rather than merely to copy a scene.[11]

Although Cole accepted other academic constraints, he also responded to more modern ideas which gave his thought a new, nineteenth-century flavor. Reynolds, in Discourse 13, acknowledged that a work of art can affect the imagination and thus set off a train of associations in the viewer's mind, but he never emphasized the subjective aspects of an individual's response. Instead, he believed that the artist should rely upon rules and the works of earlier artists for guidance. But that opening wedge, the acceptance of an individual's ability to enjoy and respond to a work for subjective reasons and to develop associations of thought based on that work, is central to Alison's theories of art. This difference made Alison part of the new spirit of individualism and Romanticism that developed around the turn of the century. At that time the importance of the artist's mind and the viewer's response assumed precedence over rules, traditions, and venerated models. According to Alison, "When any object, either of sublimity or beauty, is presented to the mind, I believe every man is conscious of a train of thought being immediately awakened in his imagination, analogous to the character or expression of the original object." For Alison, meaning was provided not by dependence on authority, reason, or even the object itself, but by the individual interacting with the object. Simple perceptions alone could not excite emotions unless accompanied by the workings of one's mind. "Matter is not beautiful in itself, but derives its beauty from the expression of MIND."[12] The great artist was one who used objects to awaken, not to govern, his imagination.

Implicit in Alison's arguments is the very modern notion of radical subjectivity, the idea that the qualities assigned to an object depend upon the viewer's experience and imagination. To get

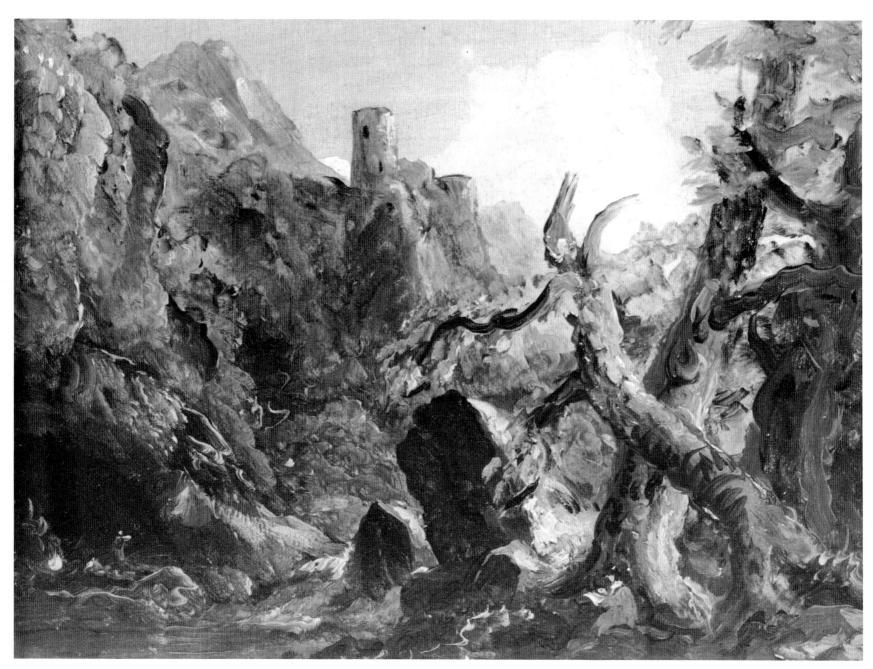

Figure 3

SALVATOR ROSA SKETCHING BANDITTI
ca. 1832. 7″ x 9½″ (18 x 24 cm).
Courtesy Museum of Fine Arts, Boston.
M. and M. Karolik Collection.

into an appropriate frame of mind to enjoy a work of art, to allow associations to flow freely, Alison believed, the viewer should be in a state of reverie or disinterestedness. He meant that a specific aesthetic attitude had to be cultivated separately from ongoing concerns, that art really was separate from life. [13] But Alison, followed by Cole, did not pursue this line of reasoning to its logical conclusion and into modern subjectivity. Instead, he tied art and aesthetic responses to old-fashioned notions of social and moral usefulness. In respect to the landscape, he thought that the beauty of a scene, say, where a battle took place, could be enhanced by specific associations with national glory. Or an autumn scene might be given increased meaning by a personal remembrance of a melancholic occurrence. "There is," he said, "not one of these features of scenery which is not fitted to awaken us to moral emotion—to lead us, when once the imagination is struck, to trains of fascinating and endless imagery." But, most important, the observation of the material world could lead the viewer to religious sentiment: "Nature in all its aspects around us, ought only to be felt as signs of his providence, and as conducting us, by the universal language of these signs, to the throne of the DIETY." [14] In brief, Alison, and Cole, tied the new interest in individuality and individual response to the traditional concerns for social responsibility and moral righteousness.

S EVERAL RECENT historians have demonstrated the influence of Alison's associationalist theories, either directly or indirectly, on American culture. [15] In fact, associationalism was to the early nineteenth century what existentialism was to the mid-twentieth, an attitude or point of view that pervaded several levels of societal thought. Examples abound in respect to associationalism's influence on nationalism and religion; just two examples will suffice. A certain John Knapp said in 1818 in a nationalistic vein: "If we take any glory in our country's being beautiful and sublime and picturesque, we must approve the work which reminds us of its scenery. If men's minds are influenced by the scenes in which they are conversant, Americans can scarcely be denied acclaim to be inspired with some peculiar moral graces by their grand and lovely landscapes. But,

moreover, it is beneficial to connect our best intellectual associations with places in our own land." [16] That nature by associationalist thinking competes with the Bible as a source of revelation is seen in Thaddeus Mason Harris's account of his tour of the upper Ohio Valley in 1803. At one point he described how his soul expanded when looking at a spectacular view: "In deep solitude, alone with nature, we converse with GOD." [17]

Cole, no less than others, automatically thought in associationalist ways. We have only to read the following lines he wrote about Mount Etna in Sicily to see how associationalism brought together thoughts on religion, the rise and fall of civilizations (in this instance, the Greek and Roman remains on the volcano's slopes), and the eternity of nature in contrast to man's measured passage on earth.

Thou art a resting place for thought,
Thought reaching far above thy bounds; from thee
To Him who bade the central fires construct
This wondrous fabric. . . . [18]

Cole's painting *Gelyna* (Figure 2), done in 1826, was an early attempt to provide the theretofore historyless and trackless American wilderness with a newly minted hallowed past by means of associating extraordinary human activities with the landscape. (As part of the semicentennial celebrations, seven novels concerned with the Revolution were published in 1825 to provide the young nation with an instant history and heritage.) The doomed figure in the painting, Edward Rutledge, was betrothed to Gelyna. After being wounded in the wilderness, Rutledge sent his friend to seek aid from the French at Fort Ticonderoga, but when the friend returned, he found Rutledge, who had struggled to a ledge overlooking Lake Champlain, dead. (It is usually thought that the ledge commands a view of Lake George, but the view from Mount Defiance, where the event is presumed to have taken place, overlooks the fort and Lake Champlain.)

Gelyna was an unusual painting for Cole. Despite his love of American scenery, he rarely sought in it specific American historical associations. His paired paintings of the 1830s, *The Departure* and *The Return* (1837) and *The Past* and *The Present* (1838), are really European scenes carrying a European content (Figures 7 and 8). Evidently, Cole believed that the American countryside could not yet support scenes of allegory or moral significance. In this respect he reflected an ambivalence similar to that of New York City's literary figures, such as Washington Irving, Bryant, and Cooper, who called for a lit-

erature with American themes but complained about the lack of historical associations in the young republic. [20] But these writers, at least, were committed to finding or inventing associations, as in Irving's *History of New York* (1809) or *The Sketch Book* (1819) or in Cooper's Pathfinder series starting with *The Pioneers* (1823). Nor did Cole emulate the New Englanders Emerson and Nathaniel Hawthorne. Both writers, the former in his essays of the 1830s and 1840s and Hawthorne in the famous preface to *The Blithedale Romance* (1852), called for the development of themes derived from local events and customs.

In his writings on American associations, Cole, at best, waffled. In 1841, for instance, he wrote that despite the beauties of American scenery, "we feel the want of associations such as cling to scenes in the old world. Simple nature is not quite sufficient. We want human interest, incident and action, to render the effect of landscape complete." [21] But in a more expansive mood he could also say, "The painter of American scenery has, indeed, privileges superior to any other. All nature here is new to art. No Tivolis, Ternis, Mount Blancs . . . hackneyed and worn by daily pencils of hundreds. . . ." [22] (Fully one hundred years later, Grant Wood was reported to have said, during another period of intense concern for the development of an American art, "There's a great future for you fellows here in the midwest. It's new, it isn't already covered with palette scrapings. Why should I have painted what a hundred artists had painted before [in Europe]? I might as well have been sending home post cards.") [23] On at least one occasion, however, Cole spoke hopefully about the future, a subject he usually treated pessimistically. Echoing a common thought of the time, he said, "American associations are not so much of the past as of the present and future. Seated on a pleasant knoll, the mind may travel far into futurity. Where the wolf roams, the plough shall glisten; on the gray crag shall rise temple and tower; mighty deeds shall be done in the pathless wilderness; and poets yet unborn shall sanctify the soil." [24]

For the actual scenery itself, regardless of associations, Cole's admiration never wavered. Before going abroad in 1829, he traveled to Niagara Falls "to take a 'last lingering look' at our wild scenery" and promised to keep it in the forefront of his mind. After his return, he noted that American skies were more gorgeous than Italian ones. Following his second trip in 1841–42, he said that neither the Alps nor the Apennines "dimmed, in my eyes, the beauty of our own Catskills. It seems to me that I look on American scenery, if it were possible, with increased pleasure." [25]

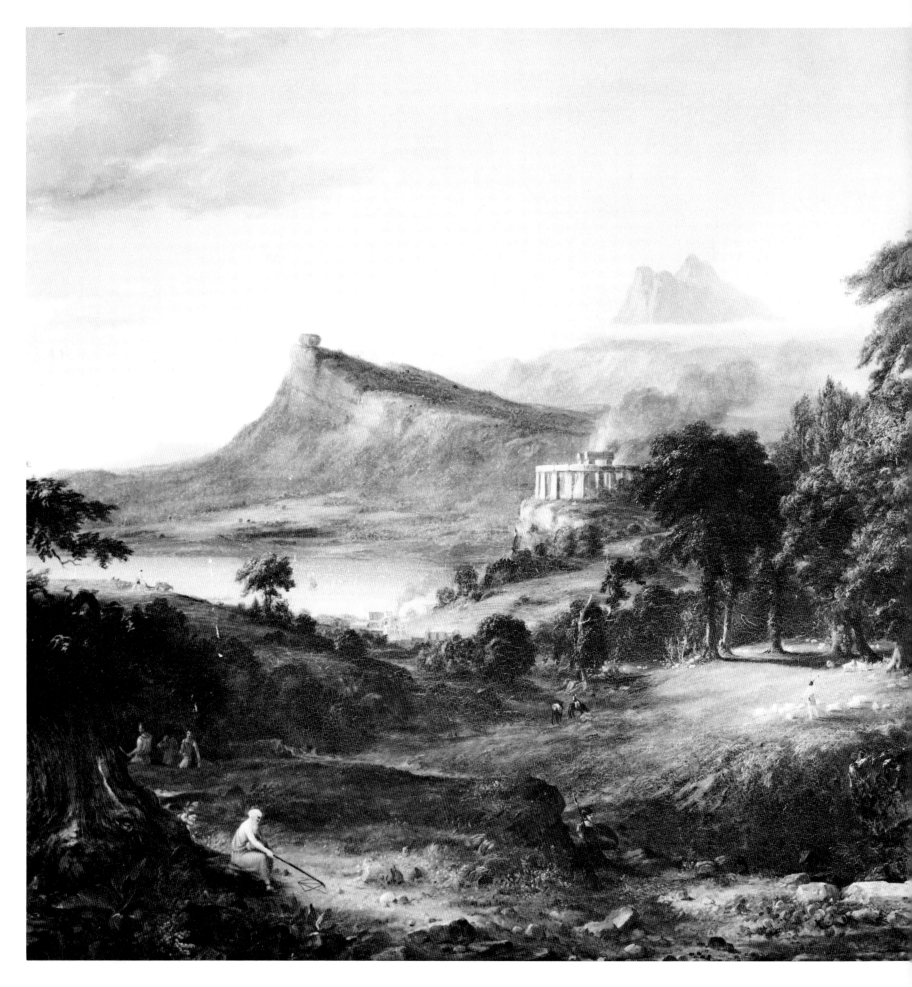

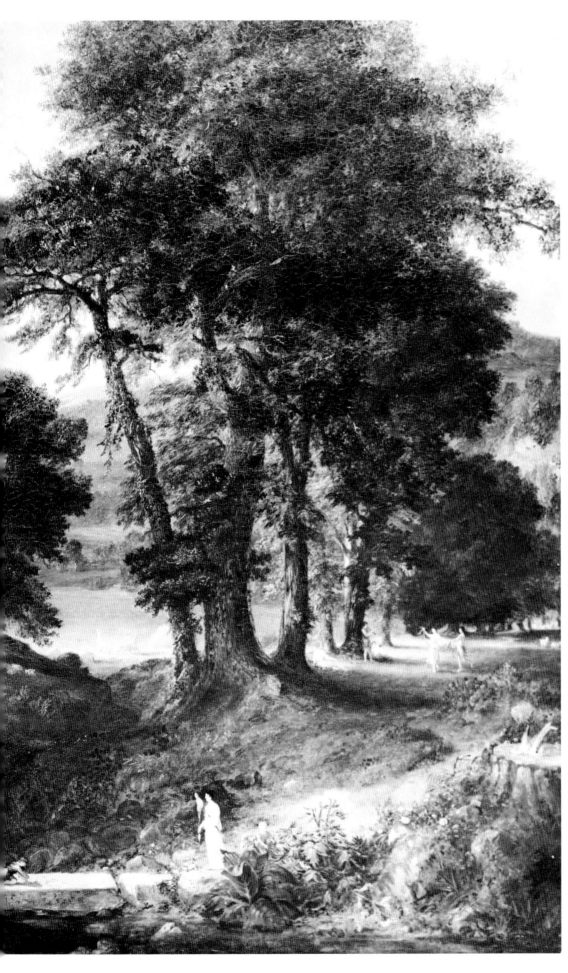

Figure 4

THE COURSE OF EMPIRE:
THE PASTORAL STATE
1836. Oil on canvas, 39½″ x 63½″ (100 x 161 cm).
Courtesy of the New-York Historical Society,
New York City.

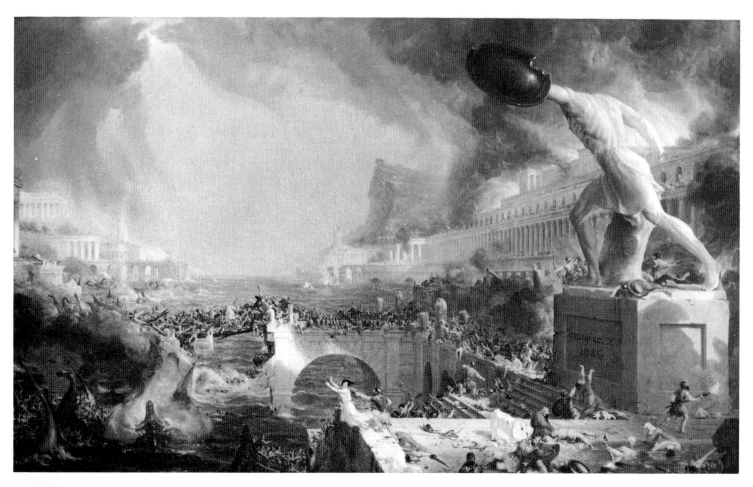

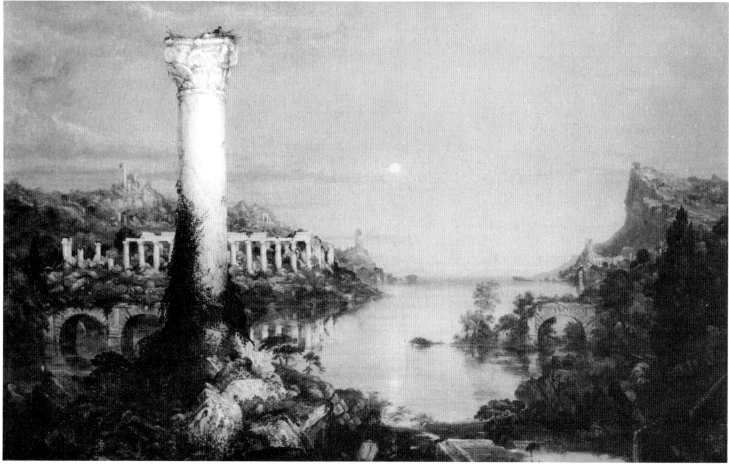

Figure 5

THE COURSE OF EMPIRE: DESTRUCTION
1836. Oil on canvas, 39½" x 63½" (100 x 161 cm).
Courtesy of the New-York Historical Society,
New York City.

O VER THE YEARS the pleasure remained acute, but the style of recording it changed. In a sonnet written to celebrate Cole's departure for Europe in 1829, William Cullen Bryant admonished the artist to "keep that earlier, wilder image bright." Of course, Cole didn't. After what seemed to have been indefatigable study abroad, his style broadened considerably.[26] With improved technique, Cole came closer to Reynolds's and Alison's advice concerning generalizations. Detail grew less insistent. Individual elements no longer competed so vigorously for attention. Horizontal movements more easily countered diagonal ones. Colors grew less harsh and forms more credibly modeled. Occasional works, such as *A Tornado* (Plate 13), still possessed the immediacy of impact of the earlier paintings, but, for the most part, Cole began to paint views from which the sense of physical intimacy was absent. Even forms in the foreground appeared smaller than before as Cole seemingly distanced himself spatially from the subjects. As a result, vistas widened and paintings included more acreage, if not to say mileage.

Cole's more panoramic focus grew, in some measure, from the panoramas he had seen when in England. Panoramas, a type of pictorial entertainment invented by Robert Barker in Edinburgh in 1787, were views, often city scenes, painted principally on long strips of canvas and viewed from a central point in a round building. Cole even made a painted sketch for a panorama in 1832 or shortly thereafter of the Bay of Naples seen at four different times during a single day. But as much as he was influenced by actual panoramas in widening his pictorial range of vision, he may also have been prompted to develop panoramic pictorial techniques in order to parallel in his paintings the panoramic literary devices used by writers such as Fenimore Cooper when describing American wilderness scenes. Cole's breadth of focus stopped short, however, of including views painted from mountaintops. Following the opinions of writers on the Picturesque, such as William Gilpin and Uvedale Price, Cole found that such views resembled maps too closely and were therefore not appropriate for an artist.[27] (Parenthetically, although Cole undoubtedly read with interest these writers' remarks on composition, landscape detail, and the relationship of

scenery to sentiment, he did not emulate their amoral aestheticism but, as indicated earlier, followed Alison by assigning meaning to his works.) When in Europe, Cole also became enamored of the idea, which he had considered as early as 1827, of creating cycles of paintings with themes based on the rise and fall of civilizations. This culminated in *The Course of Empire* (Plates 14 and 15, Figures 4, 5, and 6). Cole subsequently applied the concept to the mutability of human life in cycles such as *The Departure* and *The Return* as well as *The Voyage of Life* (Plate 22, Figures 9, 10, and 11.) After his return from abroad, he also added rural, but not village, scenes to his repertory of wilderness views. He also painted fewer religious scenes during the 1830s, even though religious imagery suffused his poems of the period. In fact, the contents of his poetry, as well as of his cyclic paintings, differed considerably from the buoyant optimism that characterized several aspects of American life. Instead, Cole seems to have tapped into the melancholic underside of the contemporary character. Whatever its sources in private musings or public events, Cole's thoughts through those years revolved around human mortality, the passage of time, the insignificance of individuals, the corruption of the wilderness by Americans, and disaffection with American business practices as well as, by extension, with the American democratic experiment.

During the 1830s and 1840s, the years of Cole's maturity, developing business interests were exploiting the country with fantastic speed. Before the depression of 1837, credit inflation fueled an enormous business boom. Between 1816 and 1840, 3,000 miles of canals were built, about 2,000 miles in the 1830s alone, and in that same decade 2,000 miles of railroad tracks were laid. As one historian has stated, land "served primarily the purposes of acquisition and ascent; it was a medium of production, consumption, and exchange distinguished mainly by its abundance and convenience."[28] Urban areas multiplied in population as well, New York City alone jumping from 123,000 in 1820 to more than one million by 1860.

None of this seemed to please Cole. He despised cities; their filth and noise aside, he said that he found a presentiment of evil in them.[29] Perhaps he associated them with extravagance or with the storied degradation of European communities. Perhaps they represented the rise of an immoral business aristocracy hell-bent on destroying the countryside that he so dearly loved. Perhaps he feared that urban dwellers, by sheer numbers, would overwhelm rural yeomen and

Figure 6

THE COURSE OF EMPIRE: DESOLATION
1836. Oil on canvas, 39½" x 63½" (100 x 161 cm).
Courtesy of the New-York Historical Society,
New York City.

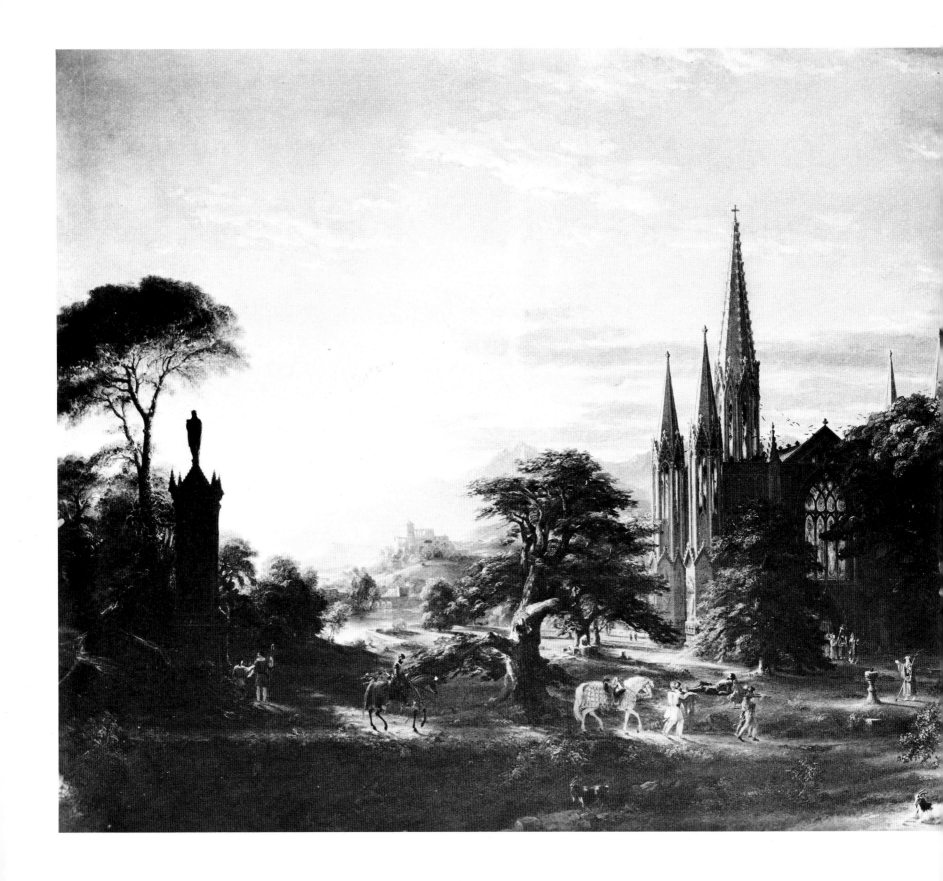

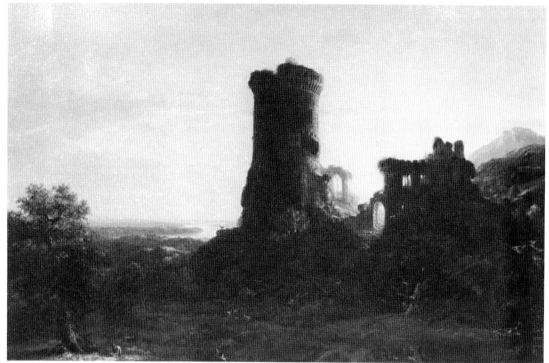

Figure 8

THE PRESENT
1838. Oil on canvas,
40" x 61" (101.6 x 155 cm).
Mead Art Museum,
Amherst College,
Amherst, Massachusetts.

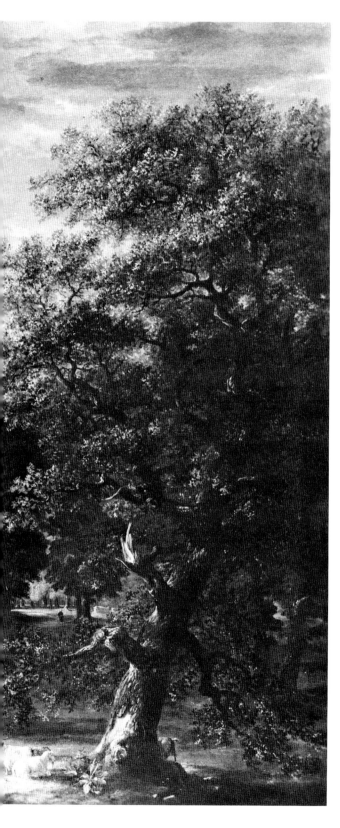

Figure 7

THE RETURN
1837. Oil on canvas,
39¾" x 63" (101 x 160 cm).
In the Collection of
the Corcoran Gallery of Art,
Gift of William Wilson Corcoran.

rule the countryside through the ballot, converting the rural paradise into an urban satrapy. In any event, he would have agreed with Natty Bumppo, Cooper's primitive Pathfinder, who was given to say, "Towns and settlements lead to sin . . . , but our lakes are bordered by the forests, and one is every day called upon to worship God in such a temple."[30]

But the temple was being desecrated every day. Cole hated the rapidity with which the wilderness was disappearing. Even during his initial visits to the Hudson River Valley in 1825, he had to endure the sight of burned-over fields, the sound of sawmills, and the stink of tanneries and tanners' wagons (see the discussion of Plate 2).[31] He increasingly disliked the strictly utilitarian manipulation of the land. "Nothing is more disagreeable to me," he said, "than the sight of lands that are just clearing with their prostrate trees, black stumps burnt and deformed. All the native beauty of the forest taken away by the improving man. And alas, he replaces it with none of the beauties of Art."[32]

This was not just the plaint of the wounded aesthete who had grown angry at the loss of several trees or whole forests, or the lament of a religious person mourning the disappearance of raw nature with its cleansing moral powers. Rather, Cole questioned and judged negatively the economic buccaneering of the Jacksonian era. Very possibly, his cycle *The Course of Empire* might have been painted in response to the American civilization of the 1830s as much as to the traditionally attributed Romantic interest in the cycles of nature, of governments, and of civilizations.

One does not have to search far or long in the contemporary literature to find beliefs similar to Cole's. For instance, the famous preacher Lyman Beecher intoned in 1829, "The greater our prosperity the shorter its duration, and the more tremendous our downfall, unless the moral power of the Gospel shall be excited to arrest those causes which have destroyed other nations." And, according to Andrew Bigelow in 1836, "We see luxury, the fatal bane of all republics, spreading and eating as a gangrene into the vitals of the state."[33]

At least two important points are to be derived from these diatribes, to which Cole heartily subscribed. First, religious influence was needed to temper greed and to control economic and social anarchy. Second, the success of the American experiment had to be based on republican institutions and virtues rather than on nascent aristocratic trappings and wealth. Wealth led to luxury, vice, decadence, and, finally, destruction. Conceivably, an American ideology based on proper republican sentiment might triumph and thus save the country from the inevitable cycle of history, an idea with roots in the Puritan belief that American civilization existed outside time. But Beecher, Bigelow, and Cole did not have much faith in that idea. In fact, Cole's cyclic works of the 1830s end in catastrophes—death and annihilation. Among artists, he was certainly not alone in reaching these conclusions. Bryant in his poems "The Ages" (1821) and "Earth" (1834) alluded to America's destruction. One might even read Washington Irving's story about Rip Van Winkle (1819) as a critique of change for the worse. Cooper's *Notions of the Americans* (1828) and *Homeward Bound* and *Home as Found* (both 1838) show societal balances still functioning during the 1820s but not during the 1830s. Indeed, several authors of the period, including Melville, Hawthorne, and Poe, so often dealt with themes of destruction and turmoil, although not always in an American context, that one may speak of an American School of Catastrophe.[34]

It would seem that Cole's responses to progress—the real kind, not the wishful-thinking kind—placed him clearly among those who had begun to idealize the simpler life of earlier times. Although his idealization links him to the outlook of Jefferson's generation, which sought a rational balance between urban and rural pursuits and between agricultural and industrial enterprises, Cole's insistent moralizing about the efficacies of nature and the evils of progress pointed instead to a retreat into a presumed golden age. He rejected the present and actually held out little hope for the future, believing that the federal union might even disintegrate.[35] His art, especially his landscape scenes, came to fulfill the public's fantasies about the good, pure roots of American life. His wilderness views became central to the pieties, not the realities, of the American present.

No wonder that to assuage their souls and to cleanse harmlessly their business-filled minds, entrepreneurs like Robert Gilmor, Jr., preferred paintings of unmolested nature.[36] And no wonder Cole objected to being considered merely a leaf painter. Perhaps he felt that giving in to clients' continuous demands for innocuous landscape paintings was a little like whoring. All the spiritual uplift viewers were supposed to extract from

Figure 9

THE VOYAGE OF LIFE: CHILDHOOD
1840. Oil on canvas, 52" x 78" (132 x 198 cm).
Munson-Williams-Proctor Institute,
Utica, New York.

Figure 10

THE VOYAGE OF LIFE: MANHOOD
1840. Oil on canvas, 52" x 78" (132 x 198 cm).
Munson-Williams-Proctor Institute,
Utica, New York.

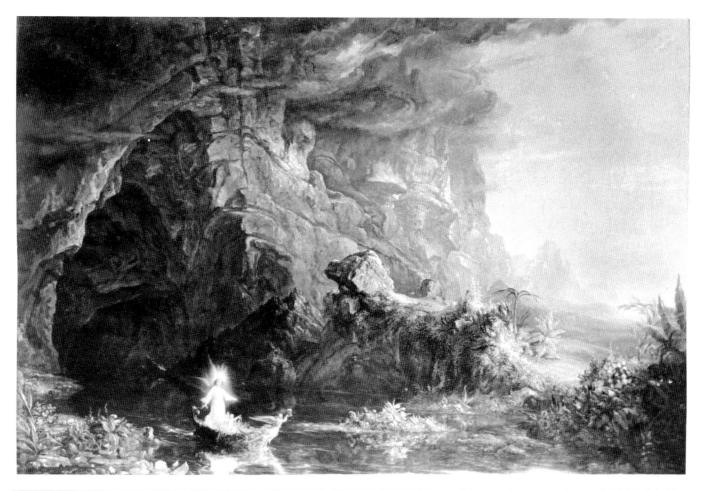

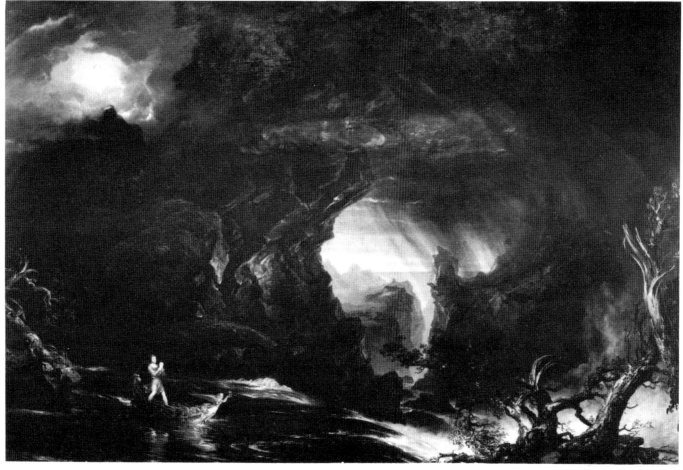

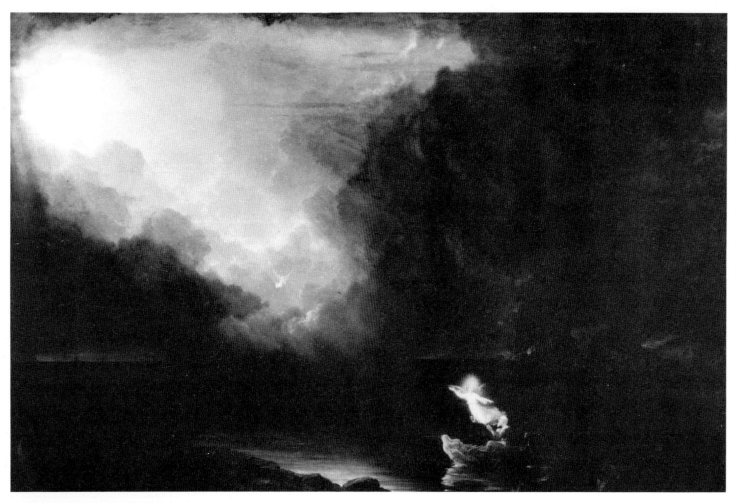

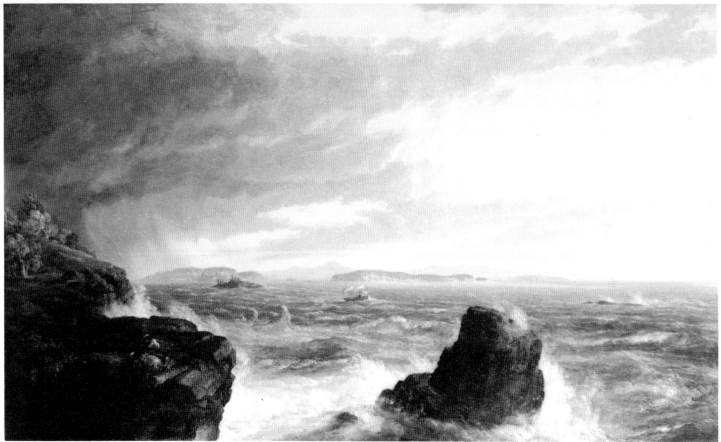

Figure 11

THE VOYAGE OF LIFE: OLD AGE
1840. Oil on canvas, 51¾" x 78¼" (132 x 198 cm).
Munson-Williams-Proctor Institute,
Utica, New York.

a landscape painting had not led to an appreciable improvement in the quality of life in America. If anything, owning such paintings relieved them of the responsibility of protecting the wilderness. Cole, a Jeremiah at heart, wanted instead to instruct and warn the public through his cycle paintings. This was a task worthy of an artist who wanted to use his art for social betterment and moral uplift. And he was embittered by the fact that he could not find sponsorship for as many cycles as he wanted to paint.

Following this line of reasoning further, we can now associate Cole with the broad phalanx of humanitarians, public and religious school educators, and organizers of uncountable "do-good" societies of the day who attempted "to extend the sphere of republican instruction in the principles of social order and virtue to the maximum number of citizens."[37] Far from being only a solitary wanderer in search of his own spiritual improvement, Cole really was a part of a broad conservative movement that tried to give responsible moral direction and leadership to the American democratic experiment.

BUT COLE WAS also, in the end, concerned with his own spiritual salvation. Given his morbid fear of the passage of time and his doubts about the survival of America, it is perhaps not an exaggeration to say that when he joined the Episcopal Church in 1842, he escaped into religion. Although he still painted landscapes, he began to concentrate on religious cycles. These included *Sowing and Reaping; Life, Death and Immortality*, a Christianized version of *The Course of Empire*; and *The Cross and the World*, based on John Bunyan's *Pilgrim's Progress*. Only the last was begun, but it was left incomplete at Cole's death in 1848. In contrast to earlier religious works, such as *Saint John in the Wilderness* (Plate 9), these later landscapes are vague and amorphous, and the sites are secondary to their religious messages. Exultation now lay in thoughts of redemption directly through God more than through witnessing God's hand in nature.

Cole's religious views, as well as his love for the landscape, have often provoked comparison with Emerson's beliefs, especially since Cole's essay on American scenery and Emerson's essay *Nature* were both published in 1836. They had surpris-

Figure 12.

VIEW ACROSS FRENCHMAN'S BAY FROM
MT. DESERT ISLAND, AFTER A SQUALL
1845. Oil on canvas, 38¼" x 62½" (97 x 159 cm).
The Cincinnati Art Museum,
Gift of Miss Alice Scarborough.

ingly less in common than one might imagine, however. Cole, in his poetry, often considered his mortality; he grew older, but the seasons continually renewed themselves. In contrast to their cyclic pattern, his was a linear one, so to speak. He therefore put his trust in God to protect him. His trust manifested itself most easily in the landscape, where he could sense God's mysterious presence. For Cole, however, God was not in nature but was distinct from it. He used nature instead to reach God. As he wrote in his poem "Sunset" in 1843:

Let us give thanks to God that in his love
He grants such glimpses of the world above
That we poor pilgrims on this darkling sphere
Beyond its shadows can our hopes uprear.[38]

Evidently, nature was not a mystery to be penetrated for its own sake, but was to be used as a guide and a teacher.

To Emerson, on the other hand, nature was a mystery. He believed that he could find God, or the Spirit of the Universe, by his own efforts. Despite recurrent bouts of skepticism, Emerson believed that he would locate that Spirit within himself; that is, God existed in him rather than as a distinct entity on high. For Emerson, nature was the mediating agent between himself and God, the channel by which God entered his spirit. Much more a mystic than Cole ever was, Emerson, especially in the 1830s, believed that correspondences existed between objects in the physical world and those in the spiritual world. To know the physical world better was to learn about the spiritual world, and the reverse was true as well. The deeper one explored one's own soul, the greater would be one's understanding of nature.

What is important is that Emerson saw matter and spirit as being on a continuum. Cole, on the other hand, believed that through matter one might be uplifted spiritually, but spirit and matter were quite separate. When Emerson referred to himself in his essay *Nature* as "a transparent eyeball," that he himself was "nothing" but at the same time could see everything, and that "the currents of the Universal Being" circulated through him, he was placing himself at the very center of that continuum between spirit and matter. He was the joining point. He could see matter and feel spirit. In his journal he once wrote, ". . . in certain moments I have known that I existed directly from God, and am, as it were, his organ, and in my ultimate consciousness am He."[39] By contrast, Cole was much more passive and traditional in his relationship with the Deity, less aggressively individual. Nature was a manifestation of God but was not synonymous with him. Cole traveled through nature to divinity. For Emerson, nature and divinity were the same, and through the one he could sense the other as an immanent force.

Cole's increasing religious concerns during the 1840s naturally affected his landscape painting. By the middle of the decade he had developed what can only be called a salon landscape manner. Works such as *The Old Mill at Sunset* and *The Pic-Nic* (Plates 26 and 28) show him catering to popular taste for pleasant scenes. These paintings appear to be genre or landscape views painted almost by rote. His late religious works, however, indicate that perhaps he would have developed a highly personal style in the 1850s, a style of old age, which, in leaving behind the issues of the day, would have become appropriately idiosyncratic and perhaps as interesting as, if not more interesting than, his earlier work. The rare waterscape, *View Across Frenchman's Bay* (Figure 12), represents this new development in his secular works. Forms are more summary, as if they were intended as background for a specific narrative content. And Cole abandoned his use of the crossed diagonals as a major compositional device. In this work, it was as if he were redefining his pictorial aims. Unfortunately, he did not live long enough to develop new ones.

H AD HE LIVED beyond the middle of the century, he would certainly have found himself increasingly alienated from other artists who had, by that time, created a brilliant American landscape tradition. Although he obviously still delighted in landscape views, his paintings had grown conventional in comparison with others. Friends of his, such as Asher B. Durand, perhaps the most typical of the landscape painters, built upon Cole's early manner in his intimate studies of forest and rural scenes. Cole's major pupil, Frederick Church, expanded the acreage of the landscapes recorded in panoramic paintings and ignored Cole's moral messages. Others, such as Jasper Cropsey, concentrated on describing the colors of the American landscape. Few were interested in weighting landscape painting with as much religious and moral baggage as Cole wanted it to carry. Less intellectual, they were less concerned with the fallibility of man and his institutions as well as less interested in extracting profound meaning from seasonal changes or even from the existence of nature itself. They were content to celebrate the landscape for less complex religious meanings and for its sheer visual splendor.

One cannot say of Cole that he painted nature simply because it was nice to look at. On the contrary, the works and thoughts of few other painters in the history of American art related so intimately to the major issues of the day. After Cole, artists and their works were peripheral to those issues, or, rather, they responded to them instead of confronting them directly. Cole painted the wilderness when it first became popular and patriotic to revel in its glories. He also recorded it not only because he believed that it gave insight into the mind of God, but also because it could serve as a locus for elevated thought and action. Coming closer to God when in nature was one thing, but using a landscape setting as motivation for personal action and uplift was another. Later artists seemed to be more content with the former.

Cole, through his paintings and writings, also faced the problem of the knowledgeable individual who, knowing the benefits of European culture, still could find praise for the primitive wilderness. That he vacillated from time to time in his statements about landscape associations and that he could write about America's brilliant future in his "Essay on American Scenery" at the same time that he was painting *The Course of Empire* attests to the complexity of his thought and the ways that it mirrored the well-documented confusions of the day. Cole provided American painting with a religious profundity and a national relevance it had previously lacked, and because of these qualities, his work was then and still is central to the ongoing dialogue between American artists and their culture.

PLATES

Plate 1

LAKE WITH DEAD TREES (CATSKILL)
1825. Oil on canvas,
27" x 34" (69 x 86 cm).
Allen Art Museum, Oberlin College.
Gift of Charles F. Olney.

Painted from sketches made during Cole's first trip to the Hudson River Valley in 1825, *Lake With Dead Trees (Catskill)* is one of the three paintings exhibited and sold in New York City that autumn which marked the beginning of his career. (The other two were *Kaaterskill Falls*, of which Plate 2 is a copy, and *View of Fort Putnam*, now lost.) *Lake With Dead Trees* was purchased by William Dunlap, author of *History of the Rise and Progress of the Arts of Design in the United States* (1834). John Trumbull, the artist, purchased the original *Kaaterskill Falls*, and Asher B. Durand, who inherited the leadership in landscape painting after Cole died, bought the third painting. After seeing *Lake With Dead Trees*, patron Robert Gilmor, Jr., advised Cole to adopt the bombastic manner of Salvator Rosa.

Although the wildness of this painting associates it with Rosa's paintings, it is essentially a topographical work with Claudian composi-tional overtones. Between emphasized framing trees, Cole arranged a zigzag leading back into space across the lake by means of a dark, diag-onally placed tree in the foreground and a bright sand spit as well as a leaning tree beyond. The dead and decaying trees, a Cole hallmark, sug-gest the passage of time. In this work they prob-ably indicate that a dam is enlarging the size of the lake, drowning the trees. As man-made or na-ture-made ruins, they might be considered the equivalent of English castle ruins, a theme often used by American poets of the day.[40] Such scenes provided the contemporary viewer with a vague feeling of sublime terror, derived, if not from the medieval past, then from the primitive present of the American wilderness. The deer in the fore-ground provide the scene with a contrasting sense of activity, but they do not interrupt the stillness of the lakeshore.

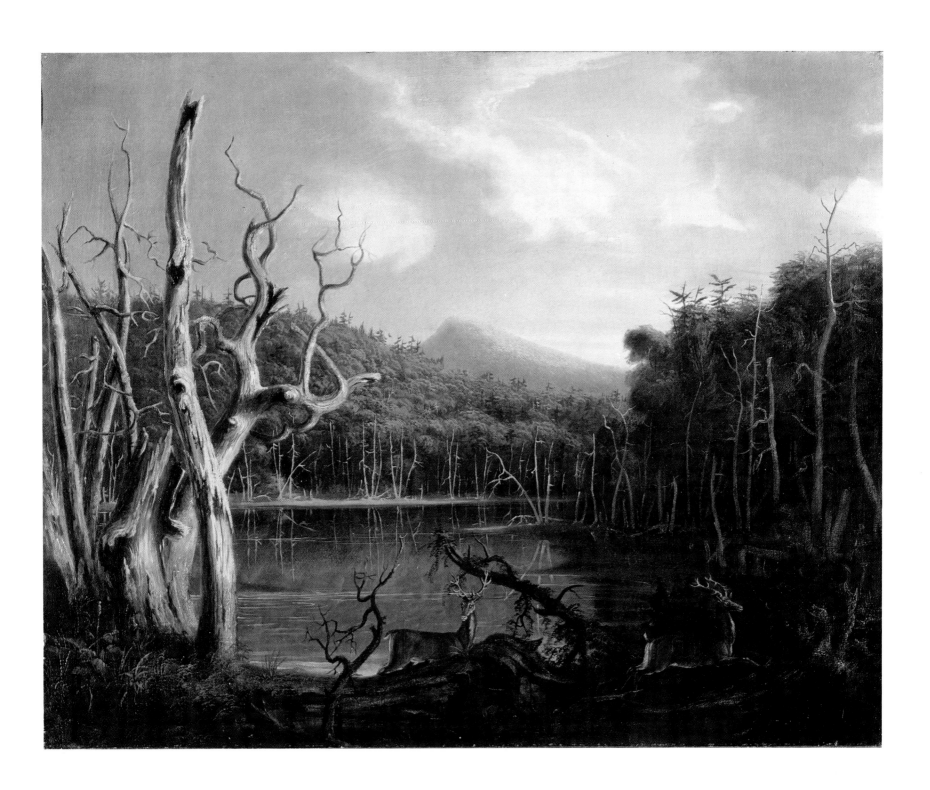

Plate 2

KAATERSKILL FALLS
1825. Oil on canvas,
25" x 36" (63 x 91 cm).
Wadsworth Atheneum,
Hartford, Connecticut.

This version, a copy of the original purchased by John Trumbull, was made for Daniel Wadsworth, an early patron of Cole's. The artist painted the scene from the amphitheater behind the upper falls. Swimming, then as now, is possible in the small pool cut by the 180-foot drop. The lower falls drop another 80 feet. Timothy Dwight, president of Yale University, visited the site in 1815, looked over the precipice, and thought that the narrow bottom appeared to be, "as it were, a solitary bye-path to the nether world."[41] But others found the area, and the falls, delightful. In 1823 the Catskill Mountain House was erected on a high ledge about three miles away, overlooking the Hudson River. The falls, downstream from a dammed millpond, were often "turned off" by the owner when he needed water power to cut logs. A favorite entertainment was to bring a group of tourists to the base of the upper falls and then turn on the water.[42] After the visitors enjoyed the spectacle, lunch was served.

Cole avoided all tourist paraphernalia in his painting, preferring instead to record the fury of the falls and the seeming remoteness of the site. Always sensitive to the character of trees and to the way they reflected the landscape in which they were located, Cole carefully depicted them around the pool's edges as if they were fighting to keep from being hurled over the falls by the strength of the water's flow. Of trees higher up mountain slopes than these, he wrote in 1828, "On the mountain summit, exposed to the blasts, trees grasp the crags with their gnarled roots and struggle with the elements with wild contortions."[43] Several artists, including Ernest Lotichius (1857), James D. Smillie (1865), and Sanford Robinson Gifford (1871), painted this falls from either the top or the bottom.

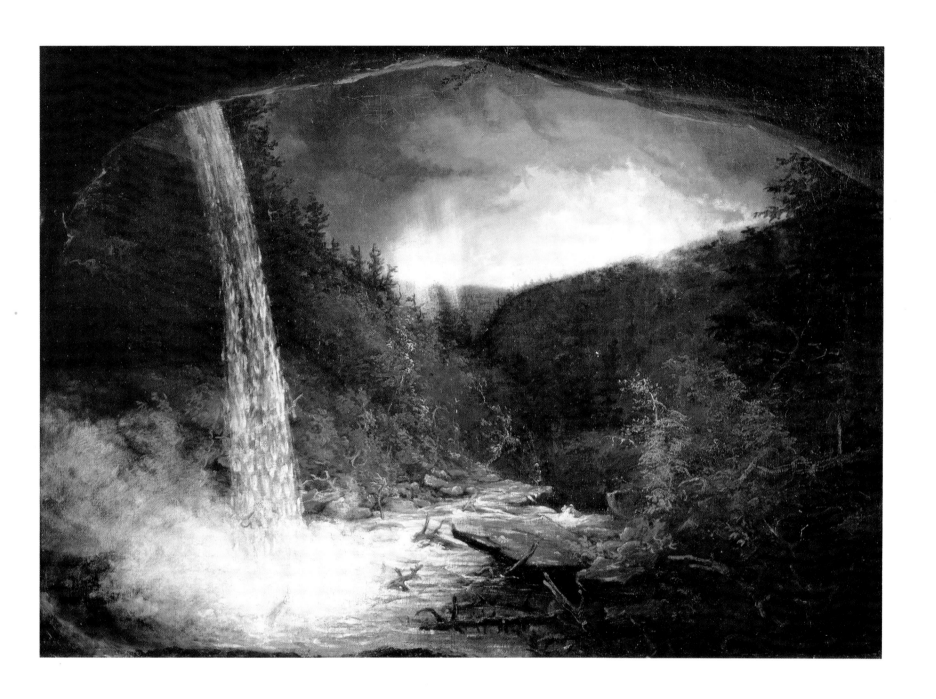

Plate 3

FALLS OF THE KAATERSKILL
1826. Oil on canvas,
43" x 36" (109 x 91 cm).
The Warner Collection
of Gulf States Paper Corporation,
Tuscaloosa, Alabama.

I have climbed up and down the gorges cut by this waterfall and the one seen in Plate 2, and I am certain that this is the waterfall now known as Haines Falls. (Area residents have also identified photographs of it as Haines Falls.) The two falls are about five miles apart. Cole labeled a charcoal-and-chalk sketch of this falls *Double Waterfall—Kaaterskill* (Detroit Institute of Art, 39.503) and a pencil study *Catskill Falls* (Detroit Institute of Art, 39.206) when the stream feeding the falls was probably still known by the name of Kaaterskill. According to the official history of Greene County, however, "Haines Falls is formed by the waters of the West Branch of the Kaaterskill falling over a precipice of 150 feet."[44] About two hundred yards downstream there is another falls. Beyond this point, the West Branch joins the main stream. *Kaaterskill Falls* (see Plate 2), which is on the main stream, is at the end of Laurel House Road, named for Laurel House, which once stood near the falls. It is located to the north of Route 23A, off the road leading to campgrounds on North Lake. (North and South lakes, located behind the Catskill Mountain House, can be seen in Cole's *View of the Two Lakes and Mountain House, Catskill Mountain Morning* [1844, Brooklyn Museum].) Haines Falls is a few hundred yards to the south of Route 23A, as one enters the town of Haines Falls from the east. A bridge now crosses the top of the falls.

Cole placed an Indian in the center of the composition to suggest the primitive, unspoiled quality of the setting as well as to give scale to the seemingly limitless spaces. He also emphasized natural aspects of the scene by including fallen branches caught on the rocky ledges.

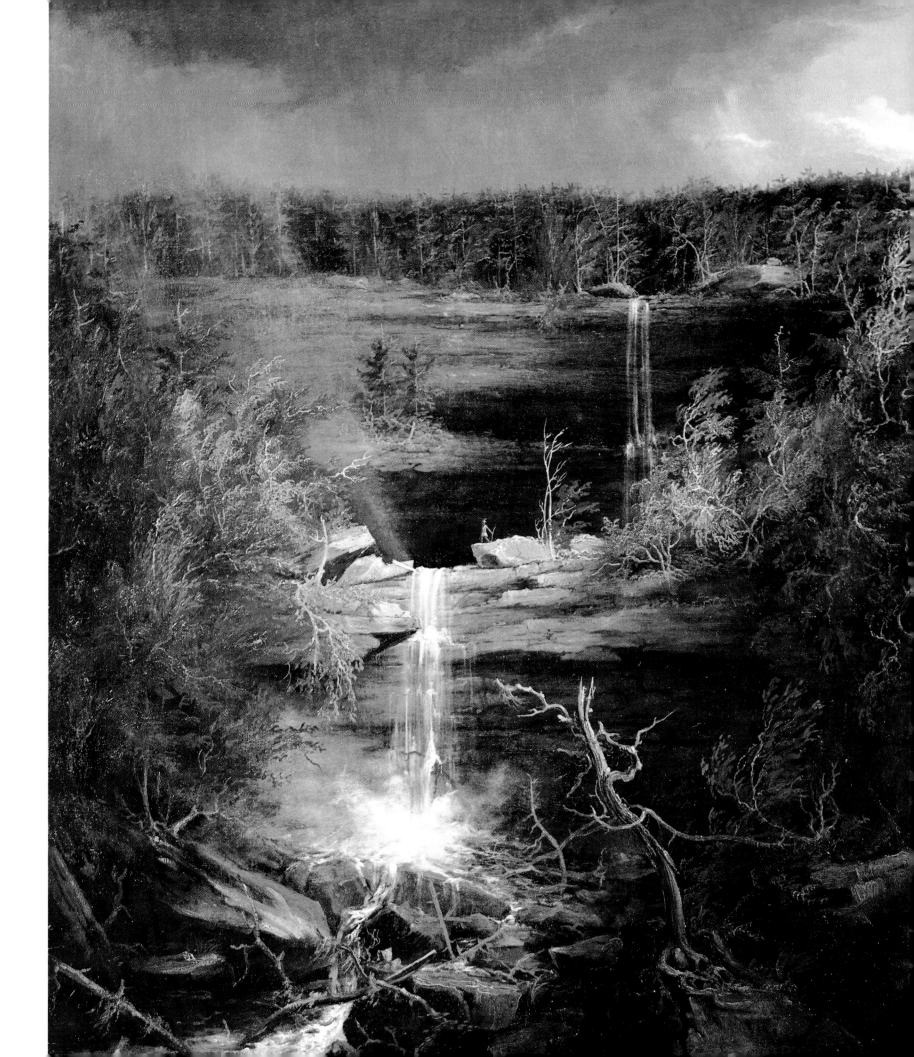

Plate 4

THE CLOVE, CATSKILLS
1827. Oil on canvas,
25" x 33" (63 x 84 cm).
New Britain Museum of American Art,
New Britain, Connecticut.

In an undated manuscript entitled "The Clove Valley," Cole wrote, "No scenery can be more picturesque than that of the Clove Valley in [the] Catskill Mountains."[45] In this painting, looking east toward the Berkshires in Massachusetts, Cole painted an advancing storm. A side of one mountain is in shadow, while on the southern face of the other mountain, autumn foliage is still brilliantly lit. As if to emphasize further the contrast between light and dark, sunlight and shadow, and, by extension, life and death, Cole placed opposite each other a cascading freshet and dead trees. Thus, the painting calls to mind thoughts about the brevity of life in contrast to nature's eternal cycles of regeneration.

William Gilpin, in his writings on landscape paintings, advised the use of blasted trees to suggest the decaying grandeur of once mighty forms. Gilpin, as well as Alison and Reynolds, generally considered that such elements should be placed in paintings of ordered landscapes, landscapes that approached the status of parks. They believed that the artist, in addition to showing the tranquil pleasures of rural nature, could manipulate such forms purposefully to awaken a pleasing train of associations. Cole, however, applied such suggestions to wilderness scenes, which he domesticated just enough to retain the look of raw nature without overpowering the viewer with the terror of peering into endless, uninhabited spaces. The terrain is rocky and broken, but it is tamed within Cole's typical framework of diagonals as well as the artifice of sunlit and shadowed areas. There is just enough sky to prevent the viewer from feeling enveloped by the forest, and the passing cloud does not threaten. As a result, this painting is both a "real American scene," which patrons like Robert Gilmor, Jr., wanted Cole to paint, and a composition, which Cole preferred to make.[46]

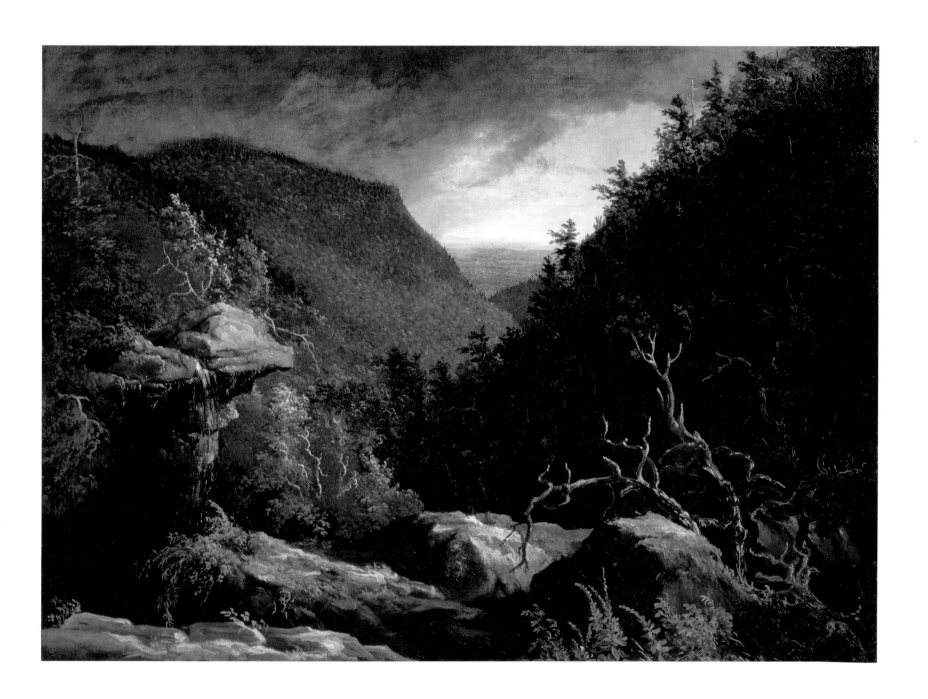

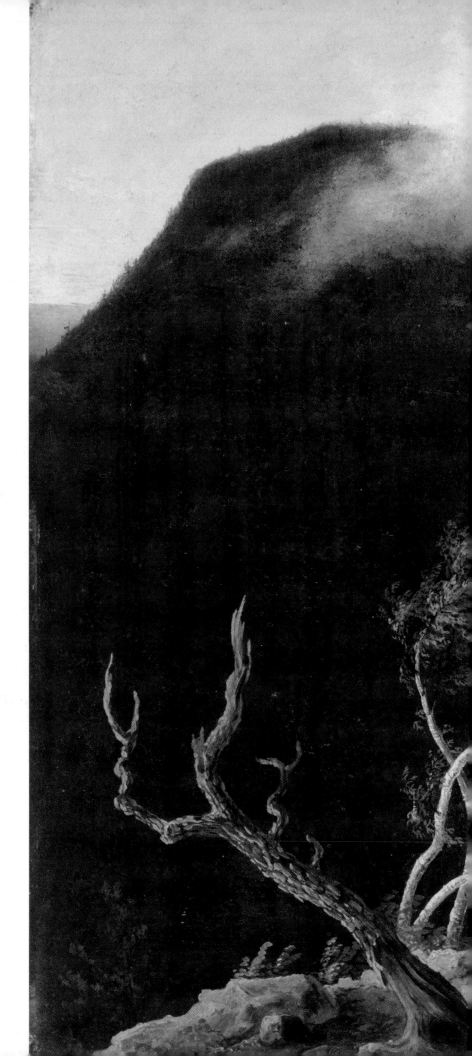

Plate 5

SUNNY MORNING ON THE HUDSON RIVER
ca. 1827. Oil on canvas,
18¾″ x 25¼″ (48 x 64 cm).
Museum of Fine Arts, Boston.
M. and M. Karolik Collection.

This painting is one of several with similar views
completed at about the same time (see Plate 4).
The site is one of the narrow, irregular coves that
open onto the plain of the Hudson River near
Catskill, the town in which Cole spent several
summers before settling there permanently in
1836. William Gilpin's remarks concerning the
paucity of sunrise and sunset scenes may have
prompted Cole to paint an early morning view.[47]
On the other hand, Cole, like any other woodland lover, did not need literary or theoretical
justification to want to paint one of the grand nature experiences, the sunrise. In his essay "The
Bewilderment," Cole said that sunshine, especially morning sunshine, makes one's spirits glow,
whereas evening suggests sadness and melancholy. (Cole rarely painted sunsets.)The last lines
of a poem, "Before Sunrise," written on October
29, 1847, point to Cole's religious associations
with this time of day:

> Be still! For in this sacred, solemn deep
> Of silence all things mute do pray
>
> Amen!

The first and fourth stanzas of another poem, entitled "Morning," further illustrate the associ-
ational process by which Cole moved quickly
from purely visual to religious contemplation:

> See how shines the morning light
> Gently on each tree and flower
> God hath kept them safe all night
> By his goodness and his power
>
> Like the Birds with cheerful voices
> When the morning lights the sky
> Our own simple songs should rise
> Unto God who dwells on high.

Cole also wrote descriptions of the sunrise, including the following:

> The mists were resting on the vale of the Hud-
> son like drifted snow: tops of distant moun-
> tains in the east [the Berkshires] were visible—
> things of another world. The sun rose from
> bars of pearly hue.... The mist below the
> mountain began first to be lighted up, and the
> trees on the tops of the lower hills cast their
> shadows over the misty surface—innumerable
> streaks. A line of light on the extreme horizon
> was very beautiful. Seen through the breaking
> mists, the fields were exquisitely fresh and
> green. Though dark, the mountainside was
> sparkling; and the Hudson where it was un-
> covered to sight, slept in deep shadow.[48]

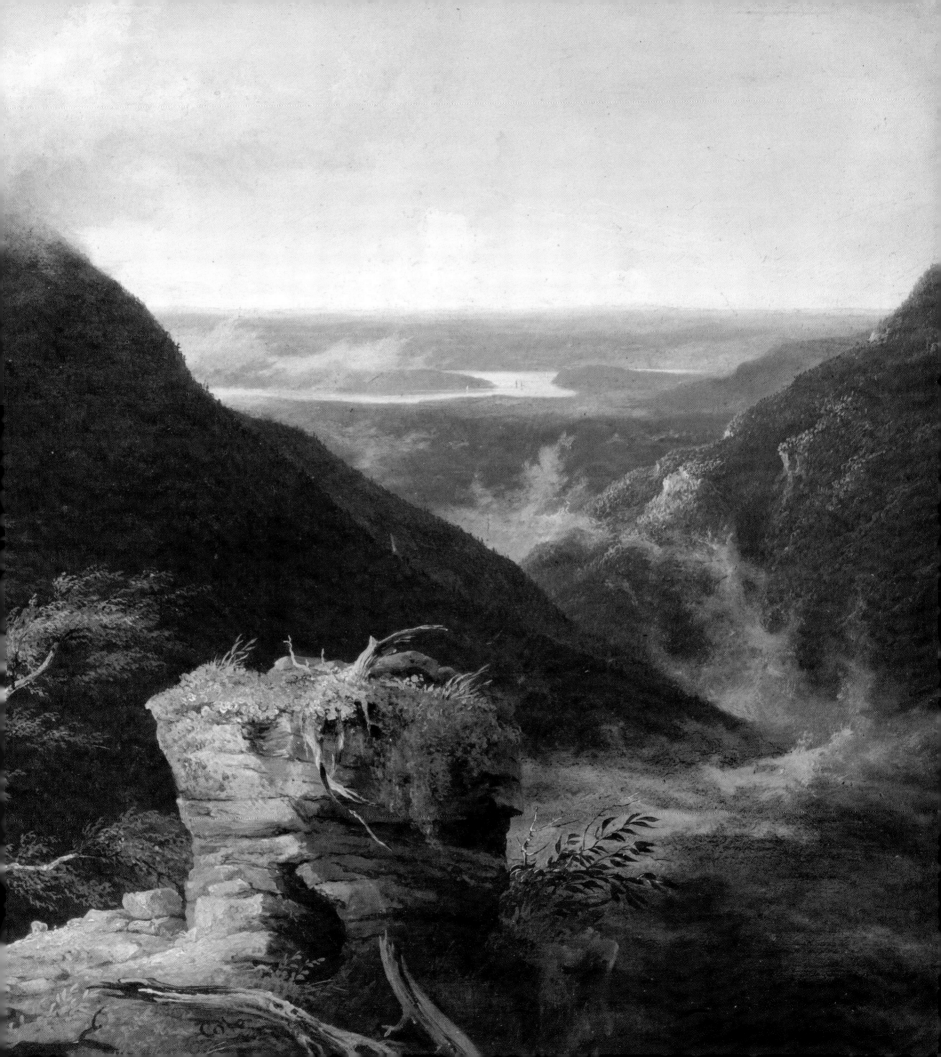

Plate 6

LANDSCAPE
(LANDSCAPE WITH TREE TRUNKS)
ca. 1827–28. Oil on canvas,
26½″ x 32½″ (67 x 83 cm).
Museum of Art,
Rhode Island School of Design,
Providence.

In contrast to several other landscapes, this view was made from the valley floor looking up to the crests of the distant mountain peaks. The perspective heightens the emotional content of what is Cole's most dramatic pure landscape painting of this period. In respect to the blasted tree in the foreground, which seems to writhe almost as if it were a living presence, Cole wrote about the effect trees produce on the imagination: "They spring from some resemblance to human form. . . . There is an expression of affection in intertwining branches, —of despondency in the draping willow." He thought that "where the region is one of savage character, the trees in their predominant traits correspond." Cole easily reached beyond this tenet of Picturesque theory, of matching a tree to its surroundings for the sake of aesthetic unity, to find a moral lesson. Commenting on trees in general, he once said, "In the American forest we find trees in every stage of growth and decay—the slender sapling rises in the shadow of the lofty tree, and the giant in his prime stands by the hoary patriarch of the wood—on the ground lie prostrate decaying ranks that once moved their verdant heads in the sun and wind."[49] Trees provoked yet another association—they were stand-ins for picturesque ruins. Walter Scott is supposed to have told Washington Irving that America's aboriginal trees were its true antiquities. Thus, speculating on the demise of a giant of the forest by fire, storm, or parasite provided an aura of sublimity for what otherwise was just another dead tree.[50]

Early works such as this one were among Cole's most popular, and patrons often wanted him to continue painting landscapes instead of narratives such as *The Voyage of Life*. William Cullen Bryant recalled his own enthusiasm for the earlier paintings when delivering Cole's funeral oration. These works, he said, "carried the eye over scenes of wild grandeur peculiar to our country, over our aerial mountain-tops with the mighty growth of forest never touched by axe, along the banks of streams never deformed by culture, and into the depth of skies bright with the hues of our own climate . . . and through the transparent abysses of which it seemed that you might send an arrow out of sight."[51]

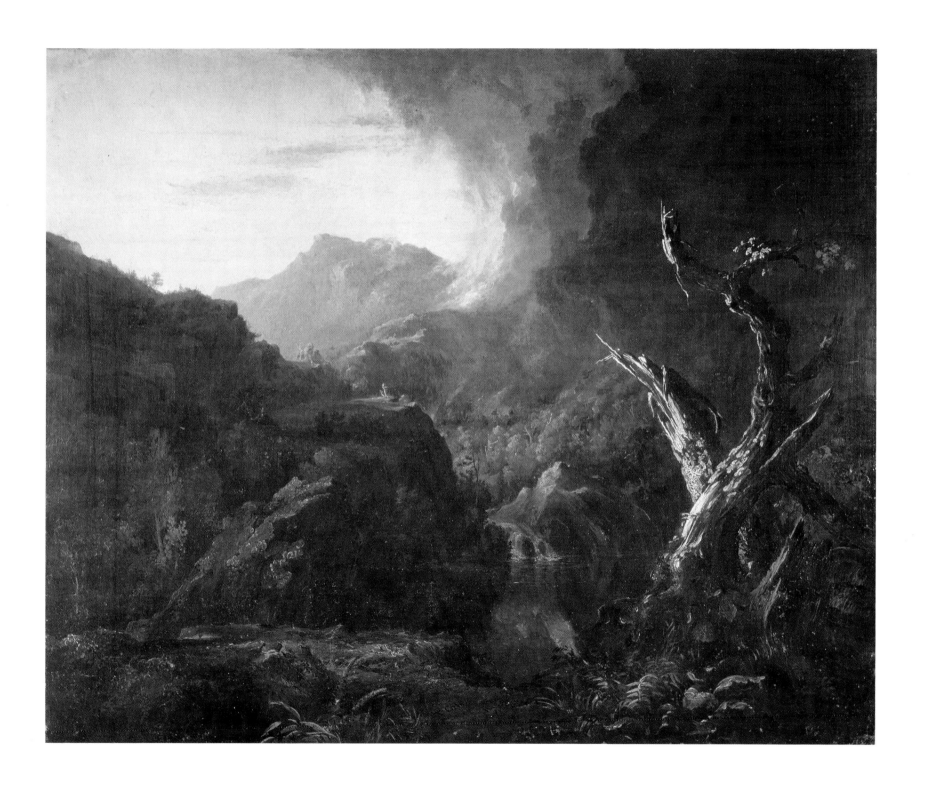

Plate 7

EXPULSION FROM THE GARDEN OF EDEN
1827–28. Oil on canvas,
39" x 54" (99 x 137 cm).
Museum of Fine Arts, Boston.
M. and M. Karolik Collection.

In the catalog of the *Exhibition of Paintings of the Late Thomas Cole* at the American Art-Union in 1848, the last lines of Milton's *Paradise Lost*, describing the sad departure of Adam and Eve from Paradise, were appended to the painting's title. The immediately preceding lines describe the landscape in which the couple would thenceforth live:

> The brandished sword of God before them
>   blazed,
> Fierce as a comet; which with torrid heat,
> And vapour as the Libyan air adjust,
> Began to parch that temperate clime, . . .

The desert images suggested in these lines, which Cole painted on the left side of *Expulsion*, were probably suggested to Milton by an ancient Jewish (Midrashic) commentary with which, since he read Hebrew, he might have been familiar. The commentary suggests that after God discovered what Adam and Eve had done, he cursed the ground, thus implicating the earth in their guilt and corruption. *Expulsion* and *Garden of Eden, a Composition* (now lost) were Cole's first paired works in which the landscape was a backdrop for religious or historical themes. Calling them "two attempts at a higher style of landscape," he gave each a distinctive quality, the tranquillity of *Garden of Eden* indicating the beautiful and *Expulsion*, the sublime. He introduced, as he said, "the more terrible objects of Nature, and . . . endeavoured to heighten the effect [of the latter] by giving a glimpse of The Garden of Eden in its tranquillity [in *Expulsion*]."[52]

Although Adam and Eve are clearly shown to be suffering for their deed, the content of the work is carried, in great measure, by the landscape. Lush foliage on the right side (the Garden) contrasts with the bleak rock formations on the left; an amiable stream meanders on the right, but a tumbling cataract rushes on the left. Winds howl, a wolf devours a stag, and a volcano explodes, a grim welcome for Adam and Eve to the world of mortals. The gate, a distinctive image in Cole's early work, is based on a similar motif in *The Expulsion of Adam and Eve* (1813) by English artist John Martin, which Cole could have seen as a mezzotint illustration for *Paradise Lost*, published between 1825 and 1827. The brilliant and intense light emanating from the gate and from the volcano's top is probably the result of Cole's experience as a painter of transparencies in Philadelphia.[53]

Plate 8

THE LAST OF THE MOHICANS
1827. Oil on canvas,
25" x 37" (63 x 94 cm).
New York State Historical Association,
Cooperstown, New York.

Cole painted the scene James Fenimore Cooper described in chapter 29 of *The Last of the Mohicans*. Leatherstocking and his companions, prisoners in the Delaware camp, watch Cora begging for mercy from Tanemund, the tribal leader. Cole painted this and an almost identical work, now in the Wadsworth Atheneum, probably at the prompting of Robert Gilmor, Jr., who had requested paintings of subjects from Cooper's novels. Cole had previously refused to complete a painting with a view of the Catskill Mountain House; not surprisingly, he placed the scene from Cooper's novel on an improbable ledge similar to the one on which the hotel was located.

Among several works Cole completed at this time which combine landscape and narrative elements, this was perhaps the first major American painting to illustrate a scene from an American novel in a landscape considered typically American. It reflected the desire, especially among New York City—based authors such as Washington Irving, James Paulding, and Cooper, to develop American themes rather than to imitate European ones, and to dignify the wilderness with a real or imagined past. (After his return from Europe in 1832, however, Cole preferred to paint works with European historical associations.) In symbolic terms, this painting can be considered to represent both a purging trial by nature and the passing of innocence, since in the ensuing action of the story, Cora, the Anglo-American, and Uncas, the last of the Mohicans, are killed.

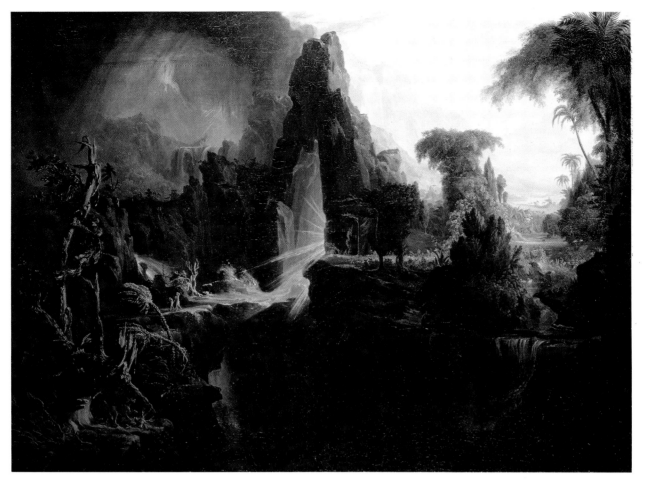

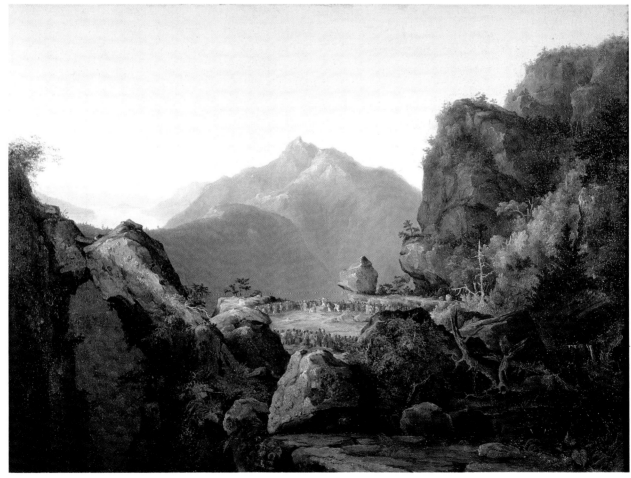

Plate 9

SAINT JOHN IN THE WILDERNESS
1827. Oil on canvas,
36" x 28¾" (91 x 73 cm).
Wadsworth Atheneum,
Hartford, Connecticut.

The imaginary landscape inhabited by the tiny figures does not possess the flavor of the Catskills. Perhaps precise topographical details would have hindered Cole's conception of a spiritualized landscape in which great religious events might take place or in which, because of its sublimity, great religious figures might exist. The grandeur of the landscape had to equal the grandeur of the religious association. As Cole wrote in his "Essay on American Scenery," "Prophets of old retired into the solitudes of nature to wait the inspiration from heaven. It was on Mount Horeb that Elijah witnessed the mighty wind, the earthquake, and the fire; and heard the 'still small voice'—that voice is YET heard among the mountains! St. John preached in the desert;—the wilderness is YET a fitting place to speak of God."[54] It is not too farfetched to think that for Cole, religious figures such as St. John could serve as intermediaries between the solitary wanderer in the wilderness and God. Aware of and overwhelmed by the immensity of nature and its total indifference to the individual, Cole may have needed to personify aspects of nature in order to bring it into some kind of relationship with himself. Just as the Greeks, and others, personified aspects of nature, so Cole used a figure such as St. John to personify religious impulses he felt when in nature.

The principal figure in *The Bard* (1817) by John Martin may have served as a model for the figure of St. John. The rock outcropping on which St. John and the figures in *Gelyna* (Figure 2) stand was a common motif and may be derived from works such as Claude Joseph Vernet's *Storm* (1787) and Philip James de Loutherberg's *Avalanche in the Alps* (1803).

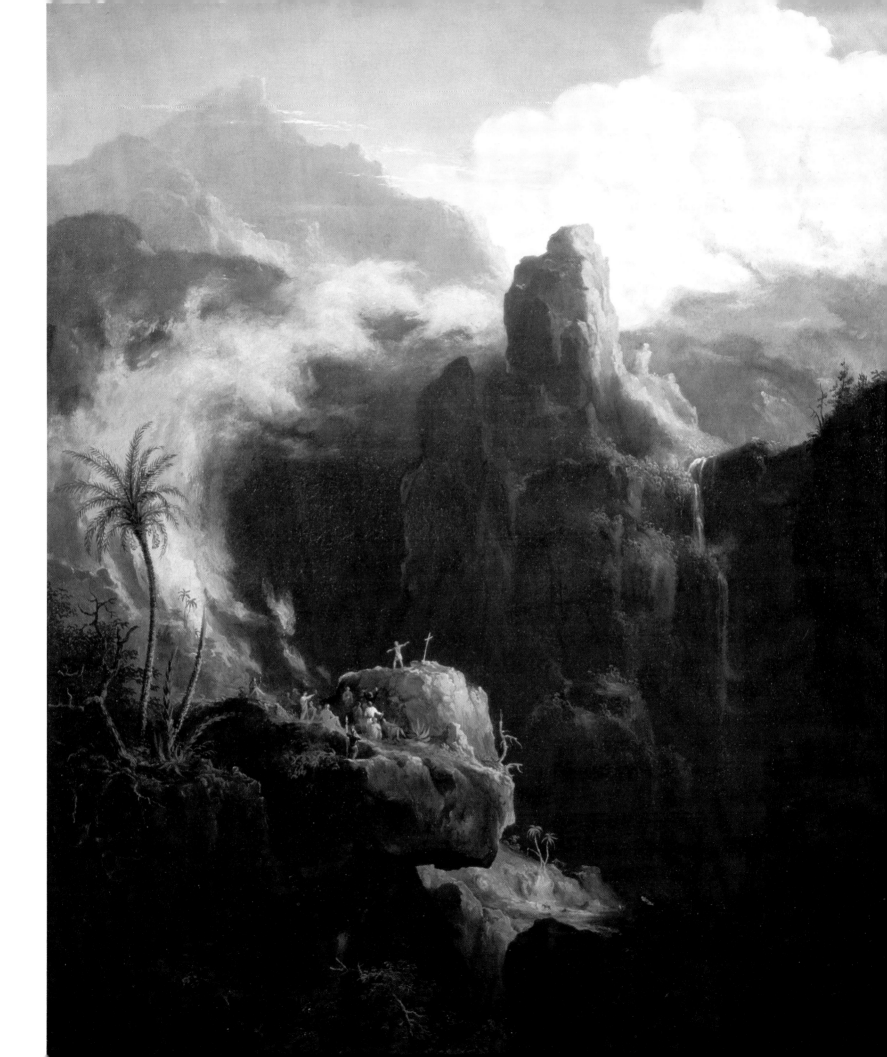

Plate 10

A WILD SCENE
1831–32. Oil on canvas,
50½" x 76" (128 x 193 cm).
The Baltimore Museum of Art.

While Cole was painting American landscapes and his first religious works in the late 1820s, he was also thinking of creating a cycle of paintings to depict the rise and fall of a civilization, or, as he said, "the mutation of earthly things."[55] Between 1827 and 1829, Cole wrote about the series in his notebooks, each time elaborating his ideas further. After going abroad in 1829, his notions concerning the rise of a civilization from savagery and its unfortunate plunge back to barbarism were enriched by his reflections on past European empires. His studies of art in London, Paris, and Italy provided him with several clues to visualize the paintings of the intended cycle. By the time he wrote a letter to Robert Gilmor, Jr., in 1832, trying to interest him in sponsoring the series, Cole had decided to show the sequence in five paintings, including savage, pastoral, and luxurious scenes, then terminating the cycle in scenes of destruction and desolation (see Plates 14 and 15 and Figures 4, 5, and 6).

Cole described *A Wild Scene*, the intended first painting in the set, in the following way: "The first picture must be a savage wilderness—the sun rising from the ocean & the stormy clouds of night retiring tumultuously over the mountains—the figures must be Savage—clothed in skins & occupied in the Chase—there must be a flashing chiaroscuro and a spirit of motion pervading the scene, as though nature was just waking from chaos."[56] All parts of the painting still seem to be in the process of evolving. Tree roots grasp at the rocks, inhabitants hunt, and the mountain dominating the harbor looks as if it has not yet reached its completed form.

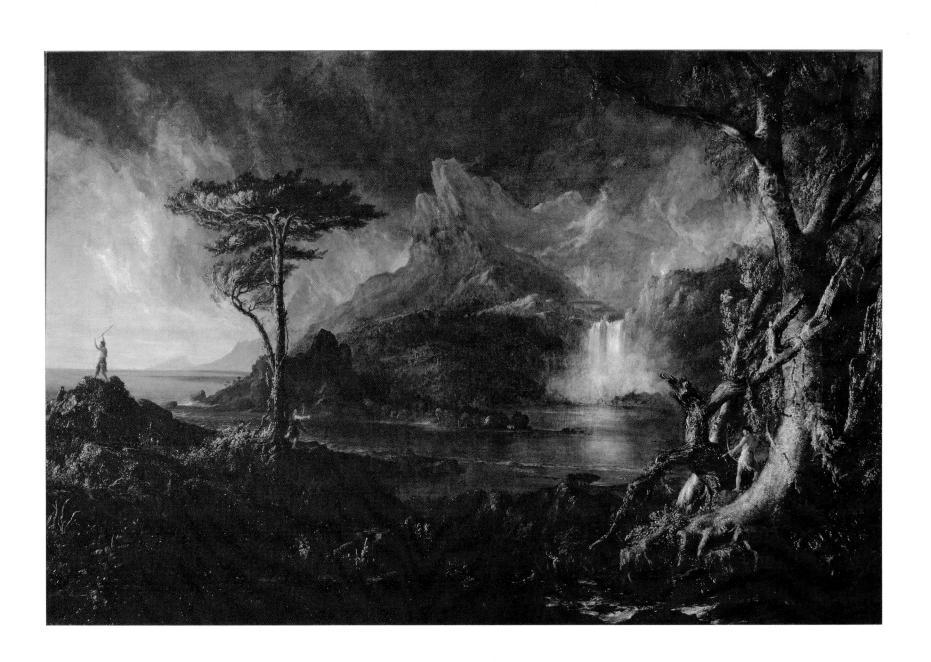

Plate 11

A VIEW NEAR TIVOLI (MORNING)
1832. Oil on canvas,
14¾'' x 23⅛'' (37 x 59 cm).
The Metropolitan Museum of Art,
New York.
Rogers Fund, 1903.

One of several scenes of ruins Cole painted during or after his trip abroad, *A View Near Tivoli (Morning)* and included a bridge and part of the aqueduct called the Arch of Nero. This painting reveals the lessons Cole learned from his study of European art. Forms are smaller in scale than before, permitting a greater breadth of space to envelop objects in the near and middle distances. Individual trees and bushes no longer compete with one another for attention but are more adroitly organized into broad arcs and contained within long arabesques that reach across the picture surface. Colors are moderated, more subtle in their tonal and spectral diffusion. In place of the ruined trees of the American wilderness, Cole could now populate paintings with the relics of past civilizations and indulge his daydreams on the mutability of life. The aqueduct has fallen,

signifying the fall of a civilization, but the mountains, or nature, go on forever. The point of the painting seems to be that only nature and God are eternal.

Preoccupied with the passage of time, Cole wrote in his journal shortly before beginning *A View Near Tivoli*, "I sat under the ruins of an old Etruscan wall, and gazed long and silently on the great scene of desolate sublimity. . . . Brief, thought I, are the limits of mortal life: man measures time by hours and minutes, but nature by the changes of the universe."[57] Cole loved Italy, especially Florence. He found the galleries there a "paradise to a painter," and even though he did not find the "natural scenery" of Italy as moving as the American wilderness, there was a peculiar softness and beauty in Italian skies "that did not exist elsewhere."[58]

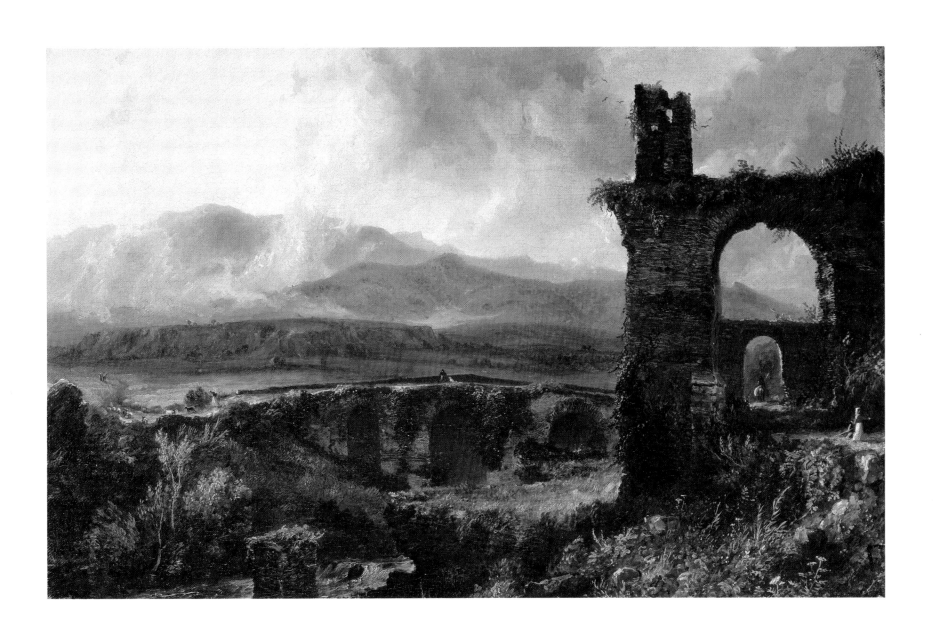

Plate 12

MANFRED
1833. Oil on canvas,
50" x 38" (127 x 97 cm).
Yale University Art Gallery,
New Haven, Connecticut.
John Hill Morgan 1893 Fund.

During the 1820s, the English poet Byron began to lose popularity in America in part because of his egotism and his opposition to traditional beliefs.[59] Yet Cole appended lines from Byron's poetry to at least three works exhibited during the 1830s—*The Fountain of Egeria* (1831, now lost), *Manfred*, and *The Course of Empire* (see the discussion of Plate 14). To the first he added lines from "Childe Harold's Pilgrimage" to complement the serenity of the scene.[60] Lines from act 2, scene 1, of the poem "Manfred" were attached to Cole's painting of Manfred's vision when the hero, disillusioned with society and seeking inner peace in the mountains, summons the Spirit of the Alps. She appears in the form of a woman standing under a rainbow.

> No eyes
> But mine now drink this sight of loveliness,
> I should be sole in this sweet solitude,
> And with the Spirit of the place divide
> The homage of these waters.[61]

Since *Manfred* and *Egeria* were hung near each other at the exhibition in 1833 at the National Academy of Design in New York City, it is likely that Cole intended to exhibit them as examples of the beautiful and the sublime. But they were not planned as a pair.[62]

Manfred is one of Cole's most violent works. In a narrow, claustrophobic alpine gorge, largely free of foliage that would soften the sharply chiseled rocks, an enormous waterfall throws up an equally enormous amount of foam. It is evident that Cole, who knew well the feeling of entrapment in a narrow gorge, who obviously remembered the deafening noises and the cool, damp, and unpleasant qualities of the air near such waterfalls, tried to create one of the most terrifying and gloomy pictures of his career. In this work, perhaps more than in any other, Cole's knowledge of the landscape and his knowledge of literature are most perfectly combined; or, to say it differently, the content and the forms are most perfectly unified.

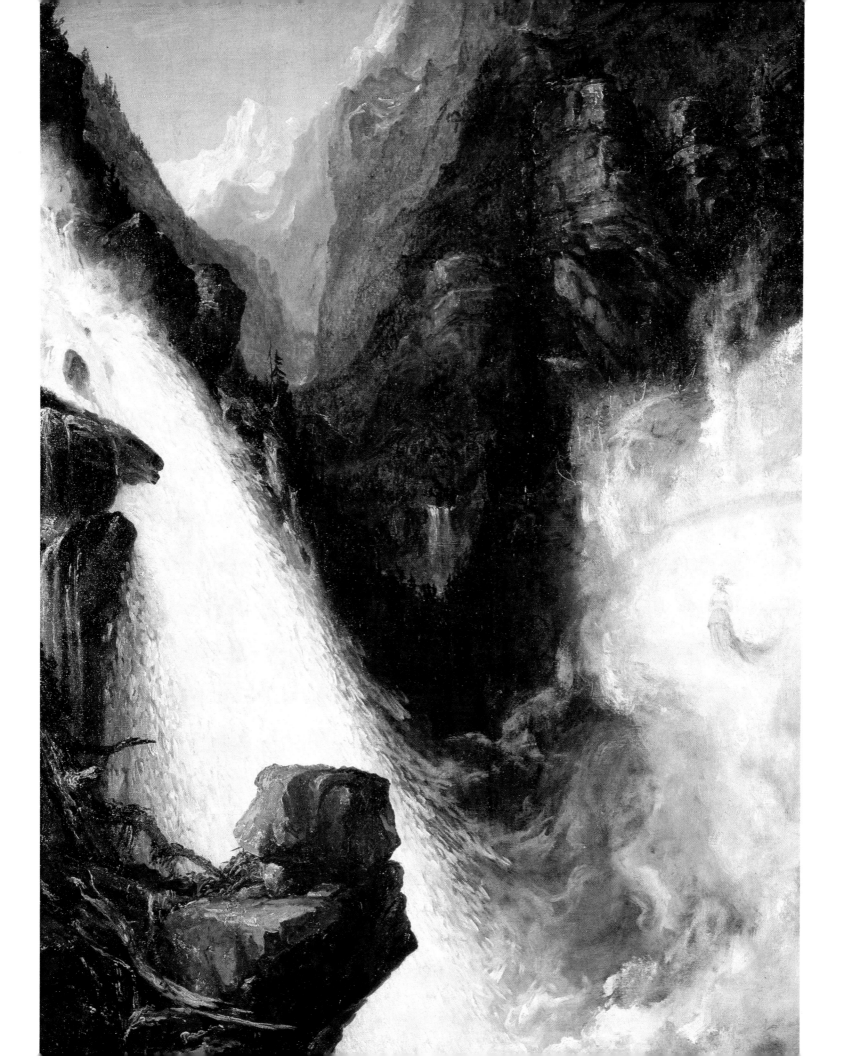

Plate 13

A TORNADO
1835. Oil on canvas,
46⅜″ x 64⅝″ (118 x 164 cm).
The Corcoran Gallery of Art,
Washington, D.C.

Partly based on a similar scene exhibited in London in 1831, *A Tornado* is one of Cole's wildest landscapes and may have been originally intended to show to Europeans in exaggerated fashion the savage nature of the American wilderness. It is also, in at least two important aspects, his most European-style landscape. First, the viewer's perspective is virtually at normal eye level rather than several feet above ground, where Cole usually located it. Second, the composition is surprisingly balanced, with blasted trees in the left foreground and wind-whipped trees in the right middle distance framing a carefully arranged central vista. It is as if Cole had adopted a typical European compositional scheme but filled it with elements from the American forest. On occasion, Cole wrote about the sublime excitement of storms. Once he said, "The storm came down in all its majesty. Like a hoarse trumpet sounding to the charge, a strong blast roared through the forest. The deep gorge below me grew darker, and the gloom more awful. A single pass of one long blade of lightning through the silence, followed by a crash, as of a cloven mountain, with a thousand echoes, was the signal for the grand conflict."[63] Ever the artist, though, Cole tempered his passions when re-creating a storm on canvas: "In the forest, during the hour of tempest, it is not the bough playing in the wind, but the whole mass stooping to the blast that absorbs the attention. . . . In a picture of such a subject detail should not attract the eye, but *the whole*."[64]

Plate 14

THE COURSE OF EMPIRE:
THE SAVAGE STATE
1836. Oil on canvas,
39½″ x 63½″ (100 x 161 cm)
The New-York Historical Society,
New York.

When Cole painted *A Wild Scene* (Plate 10), he intended it to be the first painting in this five-part cycle (see Plate 15 and Figures 4, 5, and 6). It was to be followed by scenes of pastoral and luxurious life and then views of destruction and desolation. When he received the commission from Luman Reed in 1833 to complete the set, Cole realized that he had to start anew.[65] The works were to occupy one wall of Reed's New York City residence, and Cole wanted to relate the composition, color, and lighting effects of the works to one another. The result was akin to a panorama in which basically the same view, a harbor, is seen at different times of day and season, and from slightly different vantage points as the viewer moves from left to right. The tree at the extreme left, therefore, compositionally starts the unfolding development of the empire. The sun, burning through the mist, reveals hunters, canoes, huts, and figures dancing around a fire. The useful and the fine arts are developing, and the society is in the spring morning of its life. The mountain, recognizable in each picture, symbolizes the permanence of the landscape despite the temporary changes wrought in it by man.

Several sources might have prompted Cole's meditations on the rise and passing of a civilization (see page 19), but when advertising the series, he chose the following lines from canto IV of Byron's "Childe Harold":

First freedom, and then Glory; when that fails,
Wealth, vice, corruption.

The first two lines of the canto are:

There is the moral of all human tales;
'Tis but the same rehearsal of the past.[66]

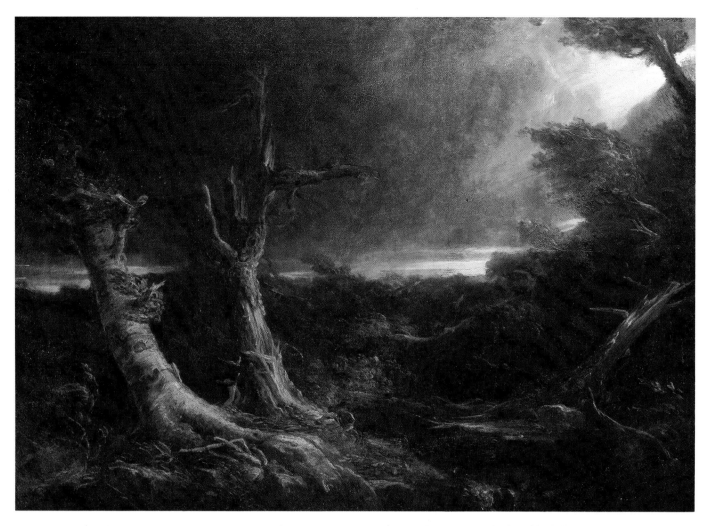

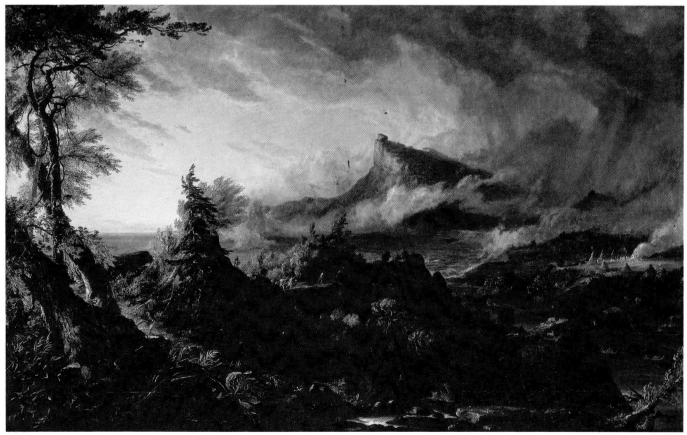

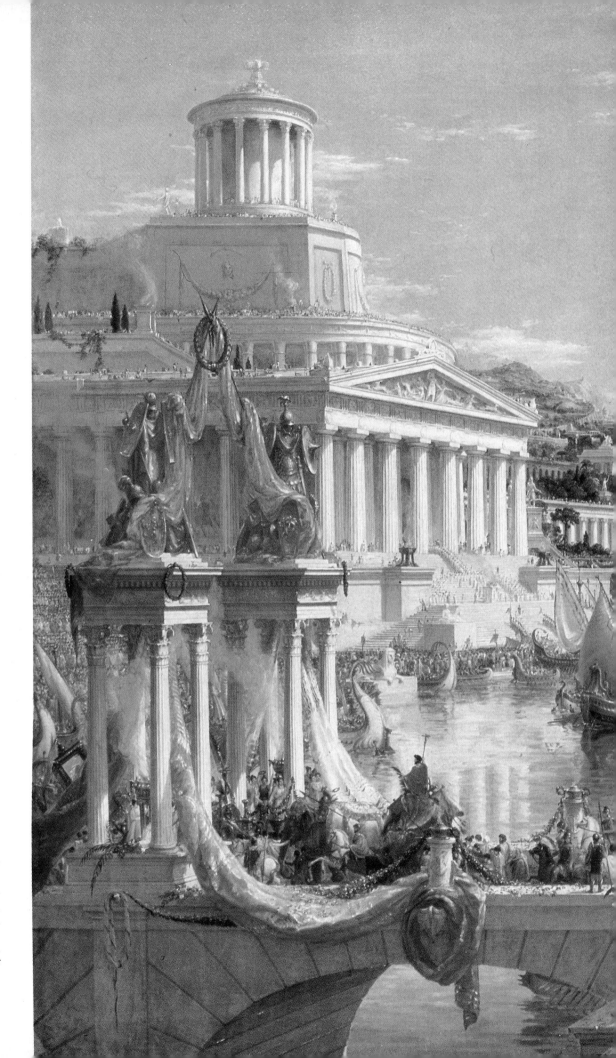

Plate 15

THE COURSE OF EMPIRE:
CONSUMMATION OF EMPIRE
1836. Oil on canvas,
51" x 76" (130 x 193 cm).
The New-York Historical Society,
New York.

Cole intended *Consummation* to be the central painting in the series, flanked by *The Savage State* and *The Pastoral State* to the left and *Destruction* and *Desolation* to the right (see Plate 14 and Figures 4, 5, and 6). He probably appropriated the idea of setting the magnificent city around a lagoon from paintings by Claude Lorrain and Turner, but to this scheme he added an almost incomprehensible amount of detail, much of it archaeologically exact and based on known sources. The triumphal procession in the foreground, the elegant buildings, and the myriad activities depict, as Cole said, "the summit of human glory," showing that "wealth, power, knowledge, and taste have worked together, and accomplished the highest meed of human achievement and empire."[67] The primitive and pastoral states have been left behind, memorialized by the pedimental sculpture in the large temple on the left. The subject, Diana and her nymphs in the chase, recalls the actual hunt in *The Savage State*. The sculpture symbolizes man's dominance over nature. In the foreground, a young bully interrupts a youth playing with a toy boat, a gesture that forecasts the wars of *Destruction* as well as characterizes the vice inherent in man.[68]

Cole's views may have reflected his opinions concerning the future of America. In his journal for August 21, 1835, he wrote that he believed the union of states would unravel and that "pure republican government" would end. "There is no perfectibility in this world."[69] Contemporaries, however, saw the series as a challenge. America need not follow the course of European empires. To these people, the belief in perfectibility overruled dismay at the prospect of another cycle of rising and falling.

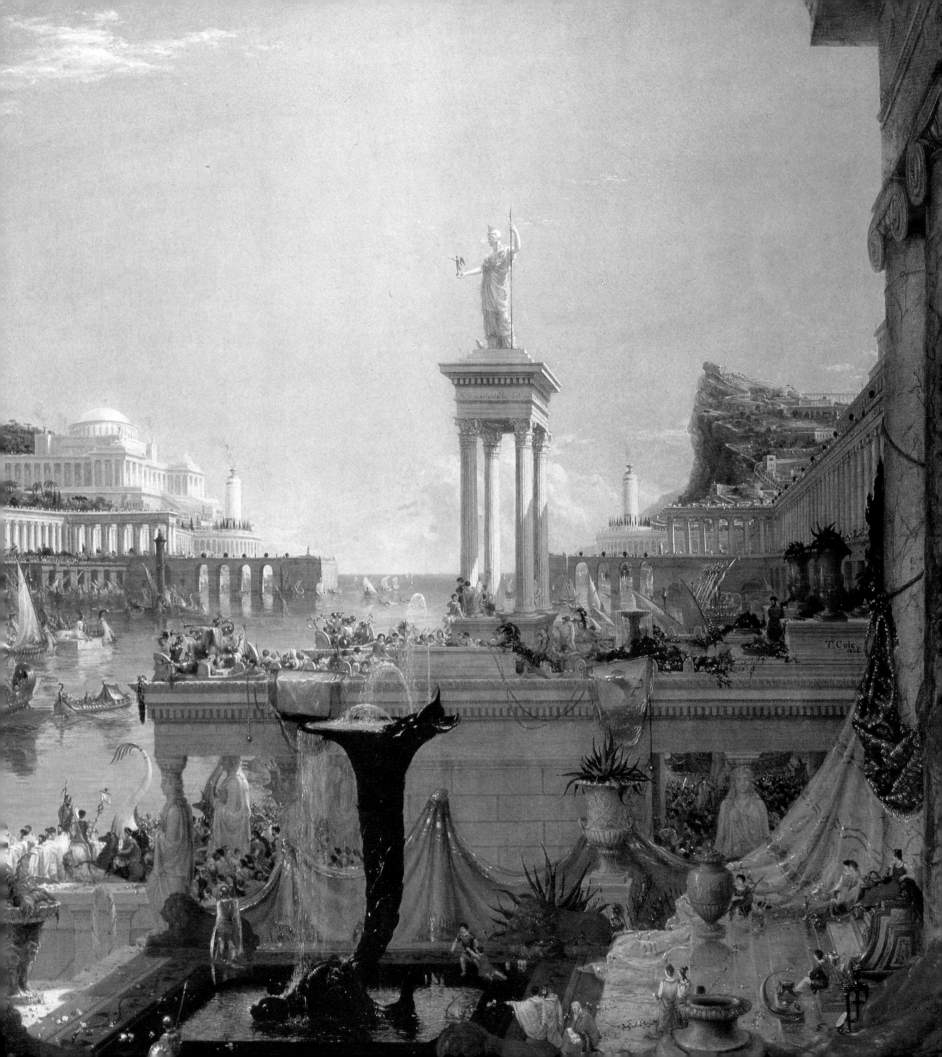

Plate 16

THE OXBOW
1836. Oil on canvas,
51½" x 76" (131 c 193 cm).
The Metropolitan Museum of Art, New York.
Gift of Mrs. Russell Sage, 1908.

A panoramic painting, *The Oxbow* is based on a double sketch in one of Cole's notebooks.[70] To the left, a storm crosses a wilderness scene. To the right, sunshine warms a rural area. Although partially stormy skies appear in several other paintings (Plates 4 and 14), Cole rarely combined such distinct cultivated and uncultivated landscapes in a single work. It is also one of the few works of his in which he acknowledges the positive qualities of progress, of turning raw nature not into a wasteland but into a pleasant rural habitat. *The Oxbow* is virtually an illustration of several lines from the contemporary "Essay on American Scenery": ". . . in gazing on the pure creations of the Almighty, he [the viewer] feels a calm religious tone steal through his mind, and when he has turned to mingle with his fellow men, the chords which have been struck in that sweet communion cease not to vibrate."[71]

But Cole probably had a totally different meaning in mind when painting *The Oxbow*. On the distant, cultivated hillside across the river there are some clear gouges that seem too obviously placed to be inconsequential. They appear to spell the Hebrew letters *Noah*, and when the painting is viewed upside down they appear to spell the word *Shaddai*, which means "the Almighty." Cole probably did not know Hebrew, but in his "Lecture on Art" he wrote, "The alphabet owes its origin to one of the Arts as may be seen in the Hebrew letters, each of which was the representation of some object, or animal, whose spoken name commenced with it."[72] If the shapes do spell the names of Noah and of the Almighty, Cole was making a direct reference to the presence of God in nature as well as to His contract with Noah or mankind. Since Cole was painting *The Course of Empire* at this time, he might have wanted to make as strong a statement as possible about living the good life according to natural (God's) law by emphasizing the benefits of the pastoral life, the life of presumed rural bliss, domestic tranquillity, and family harmony. Cole wrote at this time, however, of his fears for the stability of the country and of the vices of luxury and material lust overcoming the American people. Clearly, Americans were not fulfilling their godly promise. *The Oxbow*, therefore, was probably meant not as an optimistic statement of rural contentment but as a desperate plea to recover such contentment through a renewed contract with God.

Plate 17

VIEW ON THE CATSKILL, EARLY AUTUMN
1837. Oil on canvas,
39" x 63" (99 x 160 cm).
The Metropolitan Museum of Art, New York.
Gift in Memory of Jonathan Sturges
by his children, 1895.

A rare, entirely rural rather than wilderness landscape, *View On the Catskill, Early Autumn* is probably Cole's most Italianate American-scene painting. Here America is seen as a garden. A quiet stream meanders between framing trees in the Claudian manner, and the mountains provide a distant, gauzy backdrop. Foliage is soft and gently rounded. Cultivated fields alternate with clumps of trees in the gracefully rolling countryside. Under clear skies, a mother collects flowers for her child, and a boy in the middle distance chases horses. Nobody appears to be working, nor does the need to work trouble the leisured activities of the figures in this idealized version of rural life. Perhaps the painting is a celebration of Cole's marriage the previous year. In any event, it is a rare landscape of the "middle state"—a state avoiding the extremes of wild nature and urban existence.

If Cole's wilderness scenes showed the unique, untouched terrain from which American civilization developed, parklike vistas, like the one in this painting, show the ideal moment of that civilization, a sparkling alternative to the message of *The Course of Empire*. This painting also reveals at least one interesting parallel to the novels of Fenimore Cooper of this period, especially *Home as Found* (1838). In that work Cooper described beautiful prospects instead of dark forest interiors as in the earlier novels, clumps and belts of trees instead of unexplored wilderness.[73] His descriptions of the domesticated countryside were influenced by Gilpin and other writers who were concerned with the Picturesque. Perhaps Cole, too, was responding to similar influences at this time.

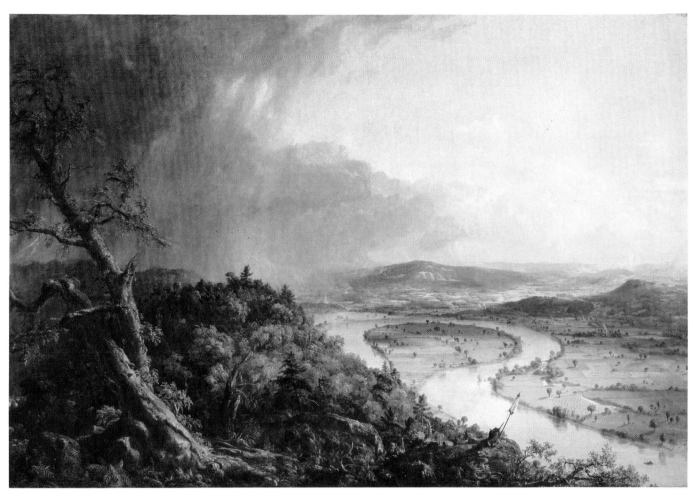

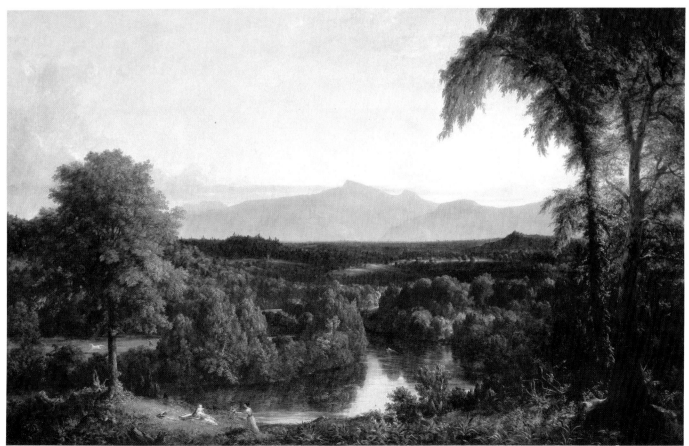

Plate 18

VIEW OF FLORENCE FROM SAN MINIATO
1837. Oil on canvas,
39'' x 63⅛'' (99 x 160 cm).
The Cleveland Museum of Art.
Mr. and Mrs. William H. Marlatt Fund.

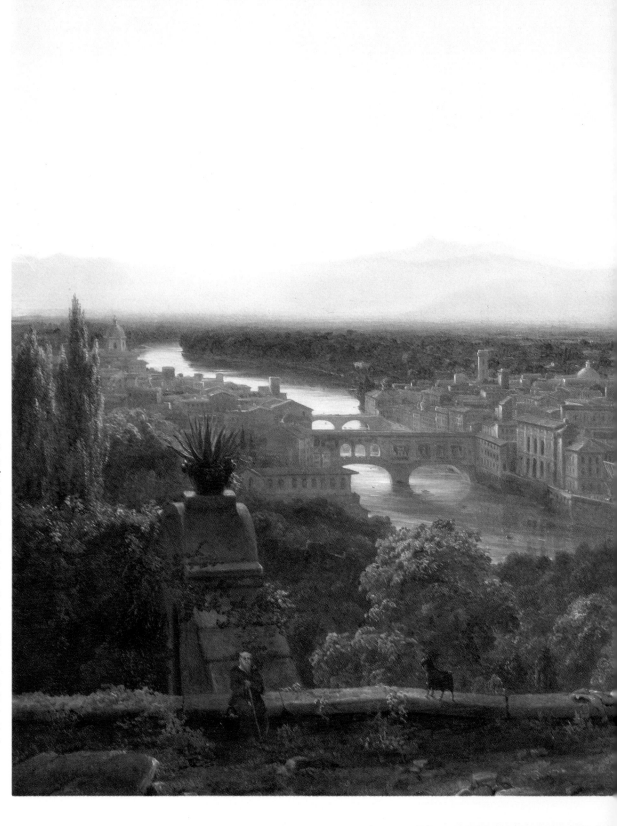

Painted in 1837, six years after Cole sketched the city from the famous overlook, *View of Florence* may be considered as a pendant to *The Architect's Dream* (Plate 23). Both represent ideal visions of humanity living in harmony with nature. Cole enjoyed Florence immensely and, in a letter to William Dunlap, contrasted its qualities to those of America. In Florence, Cole felt liberated from "the cares and business of life, the vortex of politics and utilitarianism that is forever whirling at home."[74]

On the hillside overlooking the city, Cole placed a shepherd gazing over the valley, a musician serenading three people, and a solitary figure who might be a philosopher-priest pondering the happy fate of a community that through art and religion sustains its paradisiacal qualities. Like *The Oxbow* (Plate 16), *View of Florence* is a panoramic painting, but instead of contrasting primitive and rural landscapes, it shows an urban scene consecrated to a life of thought and art as well as being happily related to its rustic surroundings.

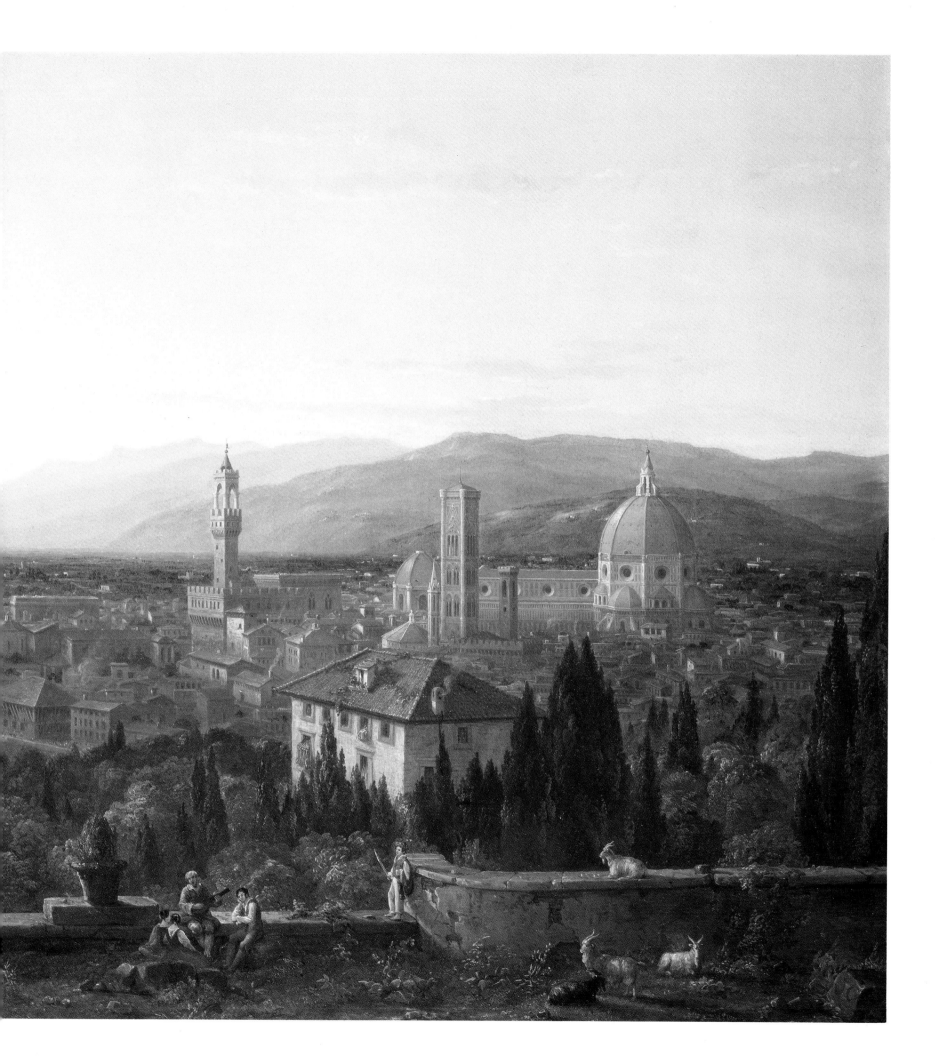

Plate 19

DREAM OF ARCADIA
1838. Oil on canvas,
38¾" x 63" (98 x 160 cm).
Denver Art Museum.
Gift of Mrs. Lindsey Gentry.

Cole first turned to Arcadian themes after painting *The Pastoral State* from *The Course of Empire* when Luman Reed suggested in 1836 that he turn to idyllic scenes. The artist completed such a work two years later and then painted several versions afterward. (Other examples are in the Wadsworth Atheneum [1843] and the New-York Historical Society [1838].) *Dream of Arcadia*, with its archaeologically correct Grecian temple, inspired by the contemporary Greek Revival movement in architecture, is a modern version of the pastoral theme that dates back to Roman literature. The inspiration for such works ultimately lies in Ovid's description of the Golden Age in his *Metamorphoses*.[75] In Cole's version, the combination of wild mountain scenery and open hillsides brings together the sublime and the beautiful. The painting represents life at its most idyllic. People live in peace with one another and in harmony with nature. They enjoy the benefits of religion and civilization without the burdens of overrefinement, luxury, and urbanization. Trees had not yet been felled, and cities did not exist. Even though the earth was not plowed, it nevertheless produced rich harvests.

Plate 20

SCHROON MOUNTAIN, ADIRONDACKS
1838. Oil on canvas,
39⅜" x 63" (100 x 160 cm).
The Cleveland Museum of Art.
The Hinman B. Hurlburt Collection.

Compared to the forms in landscapes Cole had completed about ten years earlier (see Plate 4), the forms now inhabit a less claustrophobic space. There are fewer major units, and atmospheric perspective is more gradual. Foregrounds are less encumbered with detail. Profiles of hills are more regular, bushes and trees are less individual, and prominent foreground and middleground features are less emphatic. Cole appears to have been more concerned with the grand design than with topography and was more easily able to suggest breadth of conception rather than specificity of shape. Paintings such as *Schroon Mountain* let the viewer observe the features of the American landscape without seemingly thrusting him into it, as the earlier works do. This painting is a view to be seen rather than a landscape to be experienced physically, marking a significant change in Cole's style and attitude toward the landscape that continued into the 1840s (see the discussions of Plates 26 and 31).

In other respects, this is a brilliant autumn landscape. Even though Cole had indicated that the autumn season made him melancholy (another year passing, another cycle of nature completed), he still recognized its enchantment. On several occasions he mentioned that it was the most gorgeous of all seasons, perhaps most movingly in his account of his trip to the White Mountains in 1828: "The foliage of the American forest is wonderfully beautiful in colour in the early part of Autumn. Every tint is there from the lightest to the darkest green—from straw color to bright yellow, from orange to scarlet, from crimson to purple, with all the brown olives, and these more brilliant than the artist can plan on his palette and yet often so blended and harmonized together as to make a delightful whole."[76] Cole was especially delighted with the scene depicted in *Schroon Mountain*. In June 1837, having gone on a sketching trip with his wife and Asher B. Durand and his wife, Cole wrote, "We emerged [from the forest] and our eyes were blessed. . . . The hoary mountain rose in silent grandeur, its dark head clad in a dense forest of evergreens, cleaving the sky, 'a star-y pointing pyramid.' Below, stretched to the mountain's base a mighty mass of forest, unbroken but by the rising and sinking of the earth, on which it stood. Here we felt the sublimity of untamed wilderness, and the majesty of the eternal mountains."[77]

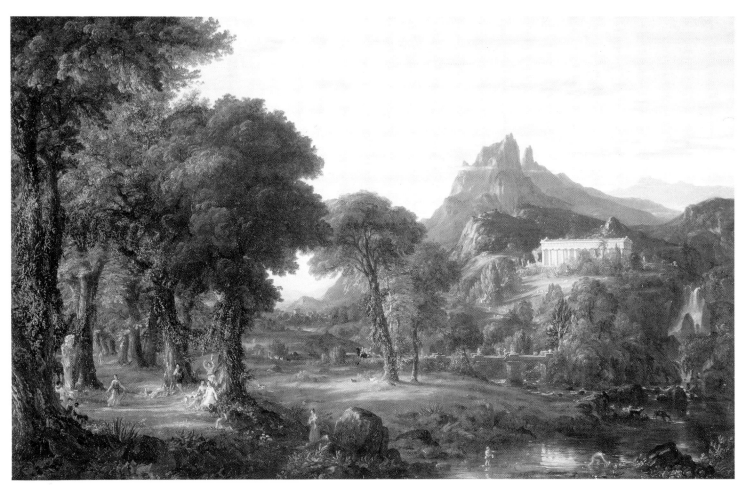

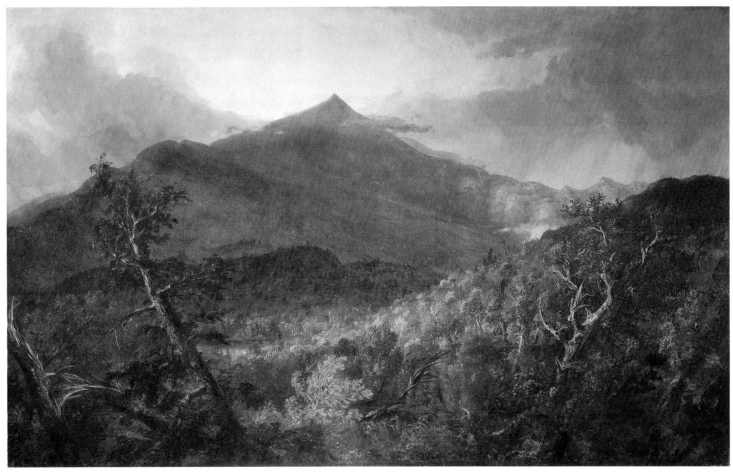

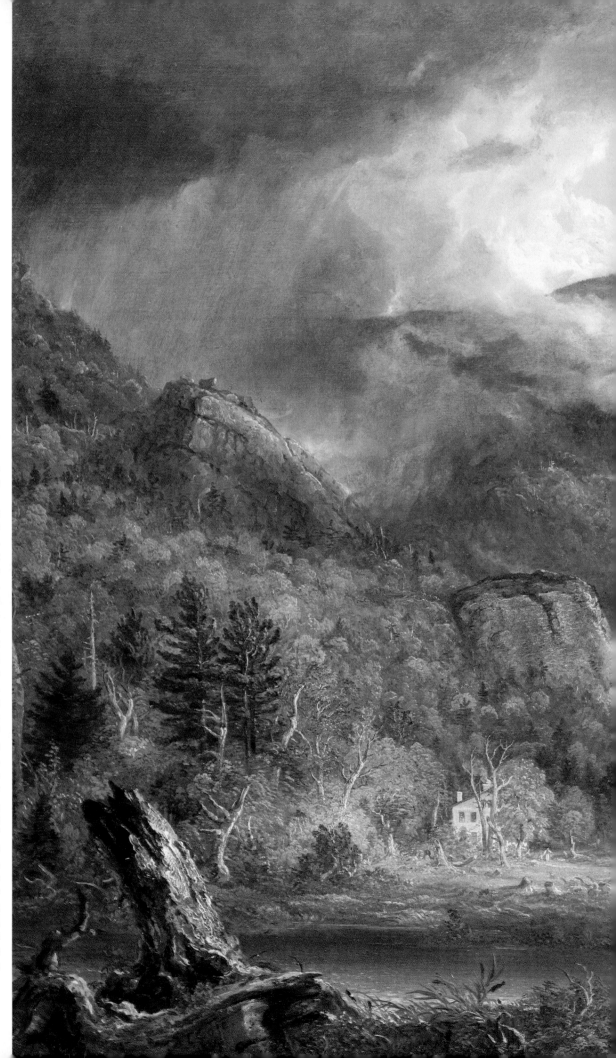

Plate 21

THE NOTCH OF THE WHITE MOUNTAINS
(CRAWFORD NOTCH)
1839. Oil on canvas,
40" x 61½" (102 x 156 cm).
National Gallery of Art, Washington, D.C.
Andrew Mellon Fund.

Although Cole lived in the Catskills, he found the White Mountains enchanting, "a union of the picturesque, the sublime, and the magnificent. . . . The traveller who passes the Sandwich range on his way up the White Mountains, of which it is a spur, cannot but acknowledge, that although in some regions of the globe nature has wrought on a more stupendous scale, yet she has nowhere so completely married together grandeur and loveliness—there he sees the sublime melting into the beautiful, the savage tempered by the magnificent."[78] Cole first visited this area in 1828 with George Platt. "[We] entered the Notch and felt awe-struck as we passed between the bare and rifted mountains, rising on either hand some two thousand feet above us. With the exception of a few curling round the airy pinnacles, the clouds had now dispersed, and the sun shone down brilliantly upon this scene of wild grandeur."[79] He visited the area again in 1839, when he made a sketch that served as the basis of this painting. By then the Notch had developed a sinister reputation. The site was that of the famous Willey Slide, which had killed the entire Willey family, and it had served as the basis for at least two short stories, Grenville Mellen's "Burned Valley" (1833) and Nathaniel Hawthorne's "Ambitious Guest" (1835).[80] "The elements," as Cole said, "seem to have chosen the Notch for a battleground, and the hoar mountains . . . appear wrinkled by recent convulsions."[81] Although Cole did not show the ravages of the slide, he did contrast the writhing, denuded trees in the plain with the fully leafed ones on the hillside. The stumps in the foreground show the violence man had done to nature.

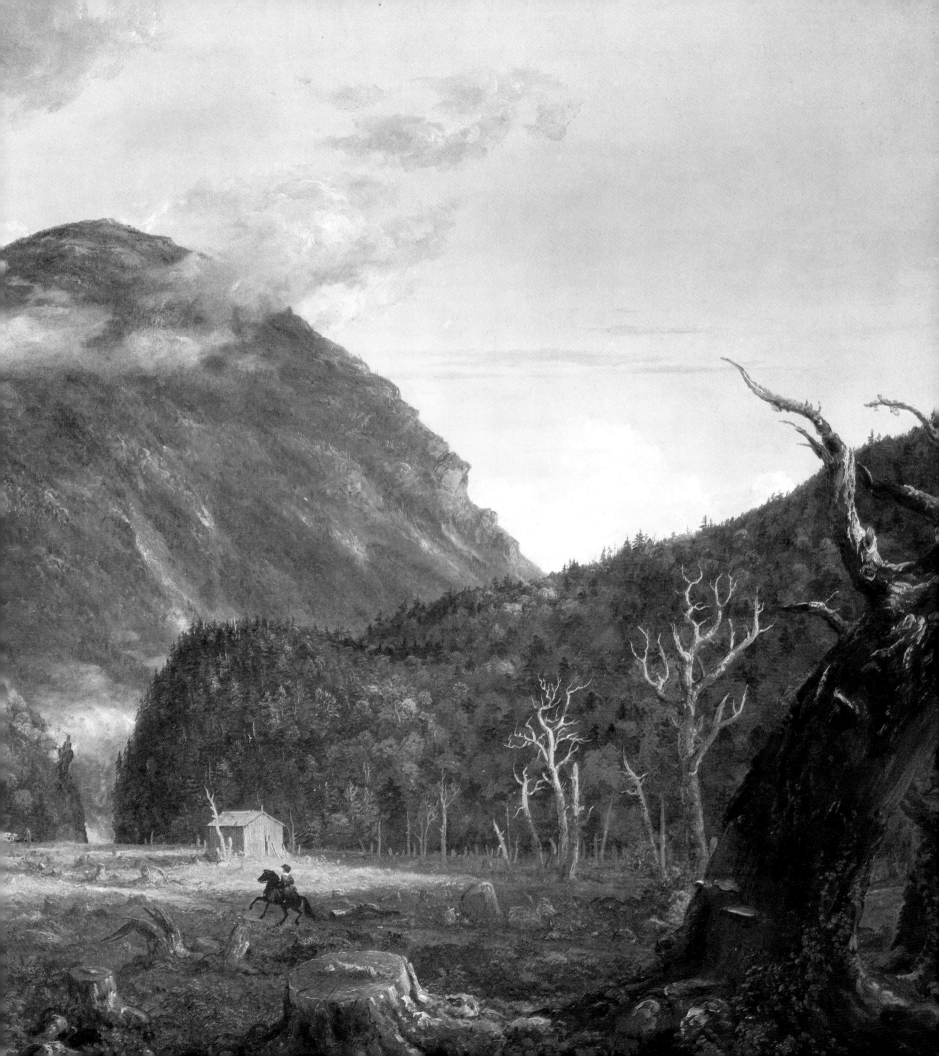

Plate 22

THE VOYAGE OF LIFE: YOUTH
1840. Oil on canvas,
52½" x 78½" (133 x 199 cm).
Munson-Williams-Proctor Institute,
Utica, New York.

Samuel Ward commissioned the four paintings of this series—*Childhood, Youth, Manhood, Old Age*—in 1839, but ironically did not live to see them completed (Figures 9, 10, and 11). *The Voyage of Life* is concerned with the stages of life, the passage of time, and personal salvation through religion. In the set, colors change symbolically from green and flowery pastels in the first work, to the sere tones of *Manhood*, to the unearthly, translucent shimmer of the heavens in *Old Age*. Foliage also varies in each panel until it disappears completely in the last one. In the work illustrated here, *Youth*, the rich landscape and the apparitional Moorish Revival building reflect the aspirations of youth. The young man guides the boat alone while his guardian spirit stands on the bank. Figures on the boat representing the hours are beautiful and intact (but in *Old Age* are shattered). The impetuosities of youth are replaced, in the *Manhood* panel, by the difficult currents of middle age and the individual's clear recognition of his need for God. In the last panel, the voyager, leaving behind the shores of life, receives a glimmer of heavenly light.

The immediate source for the set of paintings might have been a sermon by the Reverend Reginald Heber (1783–1826), its central allegory referring to "life [which] bears on us like the stream of a mighty river."[82] In addition, Cole drew on the heritage of religious dissent in England and America, best epitomized by John Bunyan's *Pilgrim's Progress*, one of the most popular books of the nineteenth century. Cole also used several images derived from popular emblem books. Their illustrations, although not always of specifically Christian content, were easily understood, and they served as a rare instance of an important artist of the period using popular, rather than fine, art sources for a major work. With *The Course of Empire, The Voyage of Life* was Cole's most popular cycle of paintings. He completed another version of it when he was in Rome in 1842. The second set is in the National Museum of American Art.

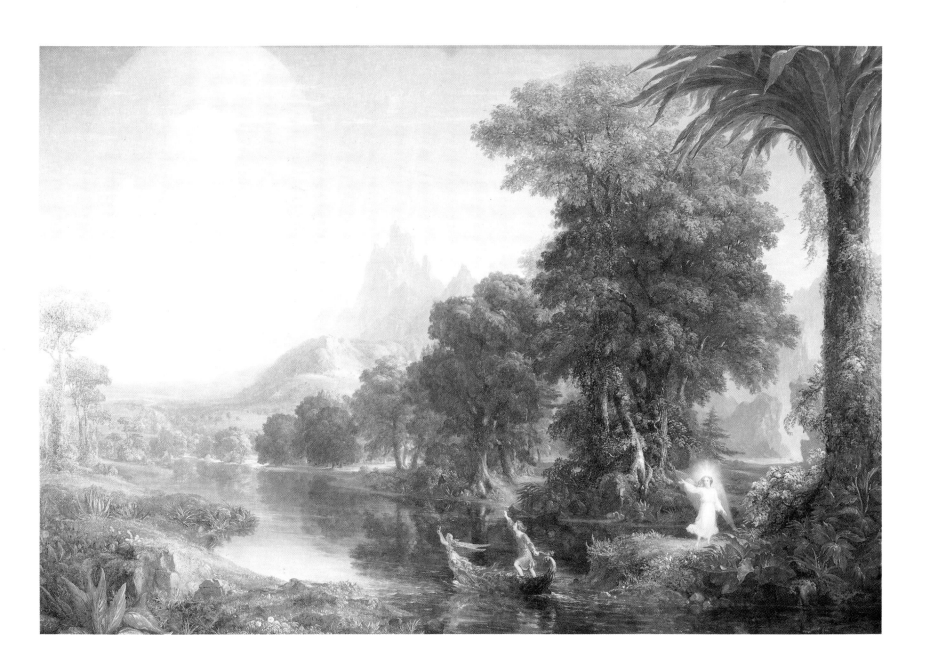

Plate 23

THE ARCHITECT'S DREAM
1840. Oil on canvas,
54" x 84" (137 x 213 cm).
Toledo Museum of Art.

Commissioned by architect Ithiel Town, this painting was returned to Cole, who would not paint another one for his reluctant client. The viewer sees, through a vaguely classical arch, an architect reclining with his books on top of a column-pedestal, looking out at buildings representing the history of Western architecture. To the left a medieval church appears in spectral shadow. Across a calm lagoon, reminiscent of works by Claude Lorrain and Turner, there are Egyptian, Greek, and Roman temples, an Egyptian pyramid, a Roman aqueduct, and a long pilastered facade topped by a dome that resembles the Ohio State Capitol in Columbus, a building erected in part according to Cole's designs. Whereas the earlier *View of Florence from San Miniato* (Plate 18) celebrates the past, *The Architect's Dream* looks to the future.

In his "Essay on American Scenery" Cole said that American associations "are not so much of the past as of the present and the future," and he alluded to the day when "temple and tower" will rise from the "now pathless wilderness."[83] Such thoughts were part of a rich and varied literature about America's future. As early as 1784, for instance, John Filson wrote of the Kentucky frontier as a recently civilized area: "Where wretched wigwams stood, the miserable abodes of savages, we behold the foundations of cities laid, that in all probability, will rival the glory of the greatest upon earth."[84]

Unlike *View of Florence, The Architect's Dream* is enframed by the arch, which limits the panoramic sweep of the landscape. Here, the buildings proceed along the lagoon into the distance, suggesting a never-ending continuation of structures limited only by the imagination of the architect and the historical vocabulary of forms he seems content to use. Perhaps such dependence on earlier styles reflected Cole's desire to rely on precedent culled from the best that the past had to offer. In this manner the architect, like the artist, fulfilled his function in society by calling to mind the highest achievements of the past as a way to guide society through the present and into the future. Such a point of view suggests a specific interpretation of the concept of Manifest Destiny—that America might become the new Rome, an improved version of European civilization, rather than a promised land for the chosen people, a new civilization separate and distinct from that of Europe. Since Cole alluded to the latter point of view in *The Oxbow* (Plate 16) and in wilderness views, *The Architect's Dream* serves to illustrate the ambiguous and sometimes mutually contradictory ways American civilization could be interpreted in the nineteenth century.

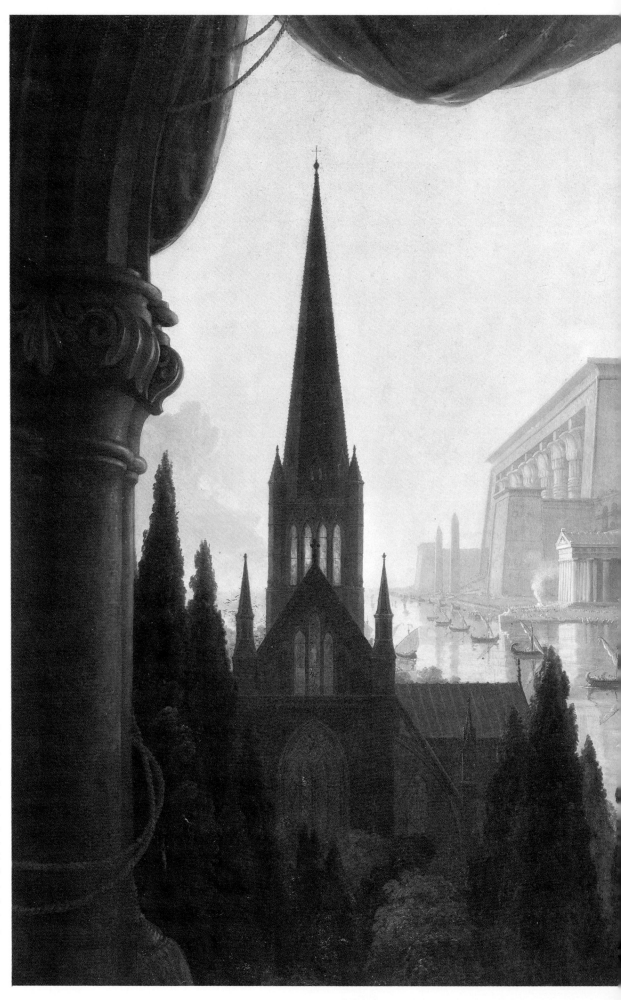

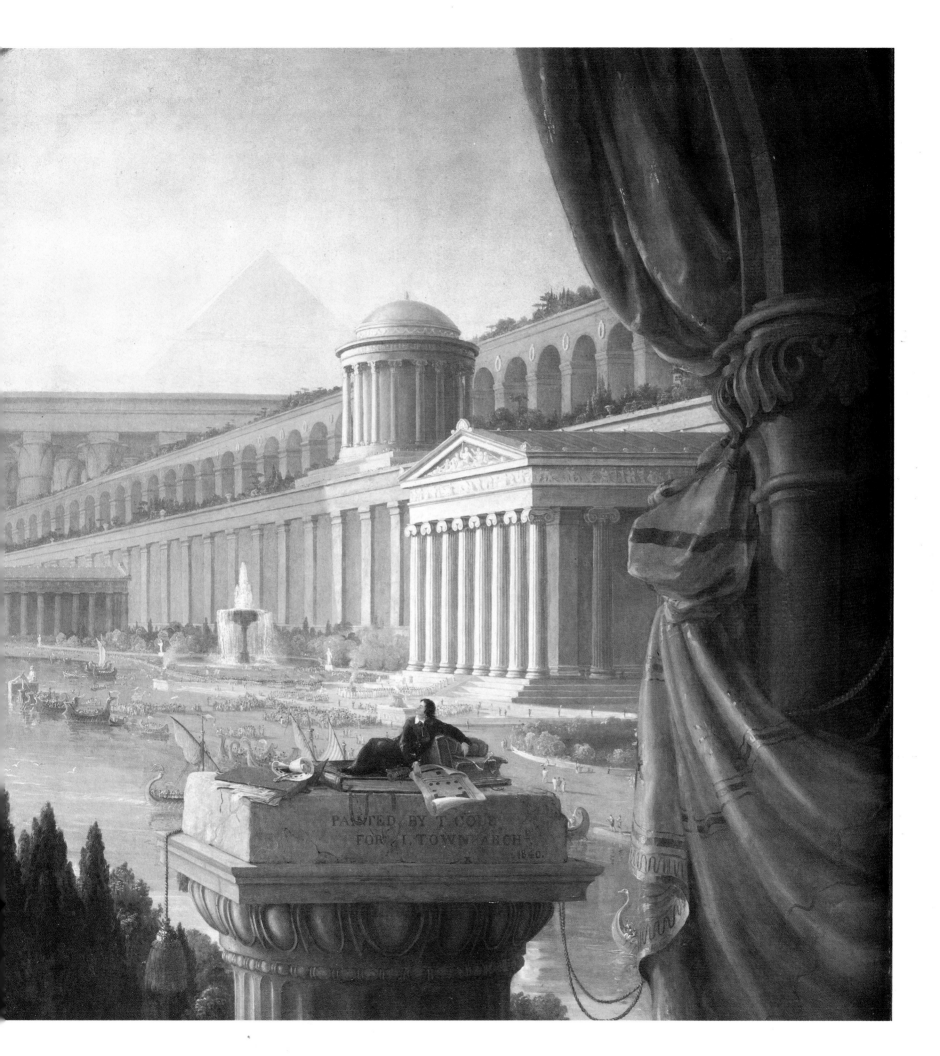

Plate 24

RIVER IN THE CATSKILLS
1843. Oil on canvas,
28¼" x 41¼" (72 x 105 cm).
Museum of Fine Arts, Boston.

With the advance of civilization, wilderness disappeared, but Cole, like others, wanted to have both. The point at which a happy balance could be struck was, of course, impossible to measure. This painting, similar to *View on the Catskill, Early Autumn* (Plate 17), indicates that the balance has tipped the wrong way. In place of a rural park there is a working farm. Trees have disappeared and, most appalling, a train has appeared. In 1836 Cole mourned the arrival of the railroad in the valley near his Catskill home. He even asked, four years later, for a debate in the local lyceum on the question "Are railroads and canals favorable or unfavorable to the morality and happiness of the present generation in the United States?" Although Cole said that he was not against progress, he did have strong reservations about the mindless destruction of the landscape and the common business philosophy guided by nothing more than the profit motive. "If men were not blind and miserable to the beauty of nature," he said, "the great works necessary for the purpose of commerce might be carried on without destroying it, and at times might even contribute to her charms by rendering her more accessible."[85]

Wanton destruction undoubtedly prompted Cole to write his long poem "The Lament of the Forest" from the point of view of moralizing trees:

> Each hill and every valley is become
> An altar unto Mammon, and the gods
> Of man's idolatry—the victims we.[86]

In contrast, Fenimore Cooper articulated the majority opinion when in 1851 in the second preface to *The Pathfinder* he acknowledged the loss of wilderness but exulted in the changes to the landscape and "the wonderful means by which Providence is clearing the way for the advancement of civilization across the whole American continent."[87] Cole's responses to technology were too bitter to consider progress as a providential occurrence. Evidently, each tree lost increased the distance between man and God.

Plate 25

THE ROMAN CAMPAGNA
1843. Oil on canvas,
32" x 48" (81 x 122 cm).
Wadsworth Atheneum,
Hartford, Connecticut.

One of Cole's most abstract paintings, *The Roman Campagna* is dominated by broad diagonal patterns composed of shadows cast by the ruined aqueduct alternating with the soft, sunlit areas of earth. These are interrupted by the dramatic verticals of the remains of the aqueduct itself, now overgrown with plants. The great open spaces to the right side of the painting, a rare kind of emptiness in Cole's work, are filled here by his reveries, if not by actual objects. Presumably, in time, the entire aqueduct will return to the earth, all traces gone of its centuries-long existence. Like the pathless and endless American forest, the aqueduct continues beyond the picture space back into history and the thoughts of the artist. There is no beginning or end to the associations the scene provokes. Just as an Indian or solitary woodsman might act as a foil for the untamed American landscape, here a shepherd, probably ignorant of the past, is contrasted with the indescribable richness of the area's history. Spatial contrast is here transformed into temporal contrast, the immensity of time substituting for the immensity of the American space. In either instance, Cole's scale is cosmic.

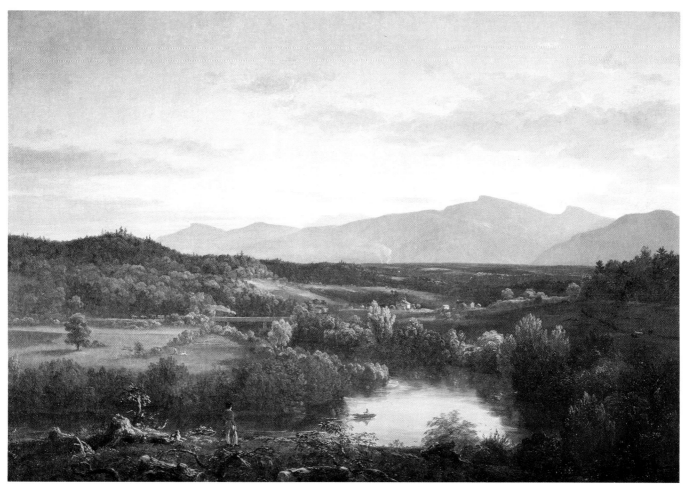

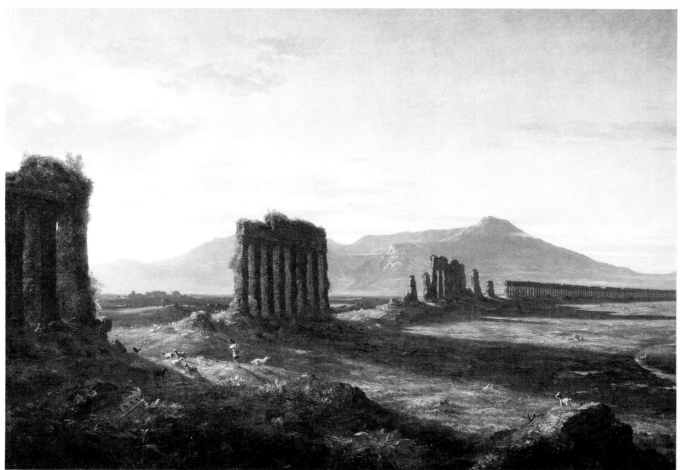

Plate 26

THE OLD MILL AT SUNSET
1844. Oil on canvas,
25¼" x 37½" (64 x 95 cm).
Collection of Jo Ann and Julian Ganz, Jr.

More than a genre scene, but less than a pure landscape, *The Old Mill at Sunset* is an exercise in portraying rural bliss. It announces that the American countryside, at least in the East, had become completely domesticated. Now America had its own picturesque buildings in picturesque settings. Trees delicately frame a vista that opens gently, with Claudian diagonals, to the distant mountains. On a less imposing and pretentious scale, this painting is an up-country version of *The Pastoral State* from *The Course of Empire* (Figure 4) in its quiet celebration of life at the end of what must have been a very pleasant day. *The Old Mill at Sunset* also represents an aspect of American painting, photography, and advertising in which rural and wilderness scenes are used to describe a place and time that probably never existed. It is an imaginative creation, not re-creation, of a time of innocence. Childhood should have been, but never really was, like this.

Of all of Cole's works of the 1840s, this one most nearly catered to the rural fantasies of his contemporaries. It is a painting for an urban public that was losing contact with the soil. With *The Pic-Nic* and *Genesee Scenery* (Plates 28 and 31), *The Old Mill at Sunset* reflects a genuine change in Cole's attitude toward the landscape. Nature seemed to stimulate him less as his interest in religious themes grew. Although his technique remained at the same high level, and, if anything, his ability to capture atmospheric effects increased, Cole began to rely more obviously on formulas and special effects. For example, in the group of trees at the left, the arc framing the vista is as artificial as anything he ever painted.

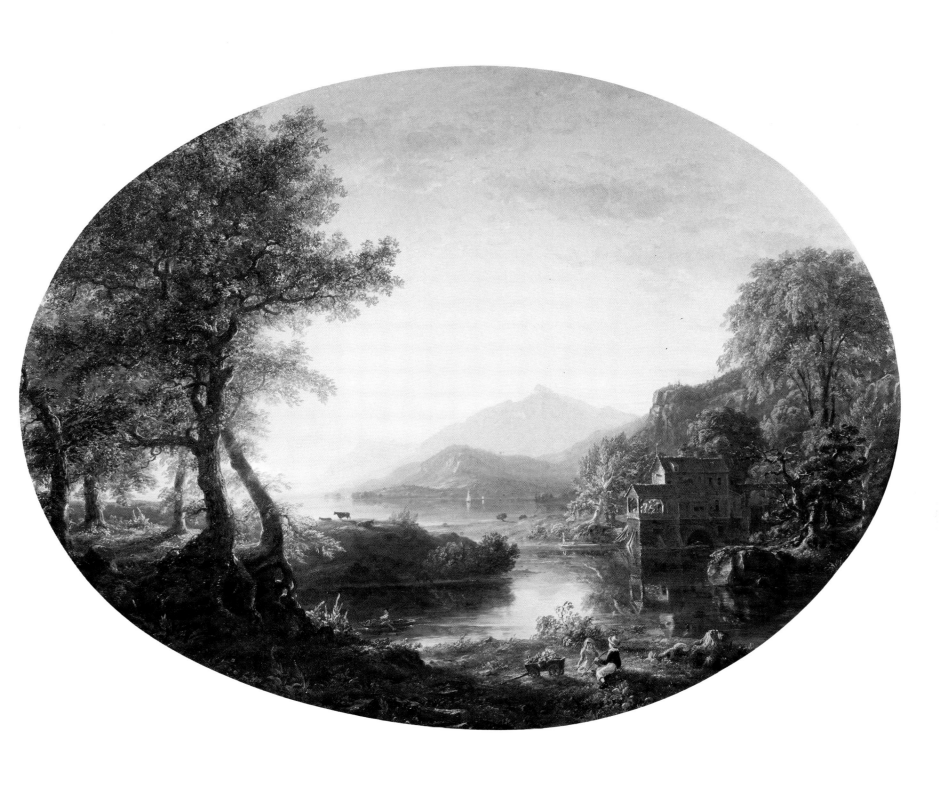

Plate 27

MOUNT AETNA FROM TAORMINA
1844. Oil on canvas,
32½″ x 48″ (83 x 122 cm).
Lyman Allyn Museum,
New London, Connecticut.

After returning from his second trip abroad in 1842, Cole wrote that "the impressions left on my mind by [Sicily's] picturesqueness, fertility, and the grandeur of its architectural remains, are more vivid, and fraught with more sublime associations, than any I received during my late sojourn in Europe."[88] Unwilling to forget the beauty of the island, he painted this, one of the grand views in Europe, no fewer than six times. Included in these views were ancient ruins, a contemporary town, the coastline, and the volcano. Technically brilliant in that Cole included accurate detail in the foreground in logical spatial continuity to the mountain peak several miles away, the paintings were nevertheless more than just topographical views of a section of the Sicilian landscape.

In a two-part article describing his travels to ancient and modern sites, Cole said, "The traveller is unworthy of his privilege, and forgetful of his duty if he extracts not from the scenes described some moral lesson or religious truth."[89] Cole then mentioned several; the finiteness of man and his civilizations in face of eternal nature was one. Cole also contrasted man-made objects with God-made objects, such as the mountain itself. He reminded the reader of the nobility of constructing buildings that possess grace and beauty as well as visual pleasure for posterity. He saw in the several ancient temples on the island the lofty attitudes of the designers who had planned the structures with such love and attention. He then contrasted the feelings kindled by these associations with contemporary canals and railroads. Pointing out the presumptions of "pride and overweaning conceit," he cautioned against the too easy path to vice and licentiousness. "Let us beware," he intoned. We are invited to join the hooded figure in the foreground of the painting to reflect upon these many lessons.

Plate 28

THE PIC-NIC
1846. Oil on canvas,
47⅞″ x 71⅞″ (122 x 183 cm).
The Brooklyn Museum.
A. Augustus Healy Fund, 1967.

Although Cole painted idyllic scenes of people enjoying themselves in a landscape setting, he rarely added the type and amount of detail that were typical of genre painting. Perhaps this work was completed in response to the increasing interest in American genre scenes and, more specifically, to the use of the landscape for vacations and amusement. In this regard, *The Pic-Nic* is an early instance of an American "vacation picture" rather than a view of the landscape or a pastoral scene with allegorical overtones. Here the landscape serves as a background for human activity rather than as the conveyor of significant content. The group of people enjoy the last moments of their picnic. The shadows have lengthened, and one imagines that a last round of songs is being completed. As a young man Cole played his flute in the woods in solitary communion with the energies of nature; he now portrays a group sing-along.

The artist struggled throughout his career to render human anatomy correctly and in this work has included more individuals than usual. Perhaps because of his concentration on anatomical accuracy, foreshortening, and the seemingly casual disposition of figural groups, he painted the trees and bushes with less than his usual flair. Their feathery leaves and powder-puff foliage are among the most artificial of his career and indicate, as in *The Old Mill at Sunset* and *Genesee Scenery* (Plates 26 and 31), that Cole's conception of the landscape had changed radically.

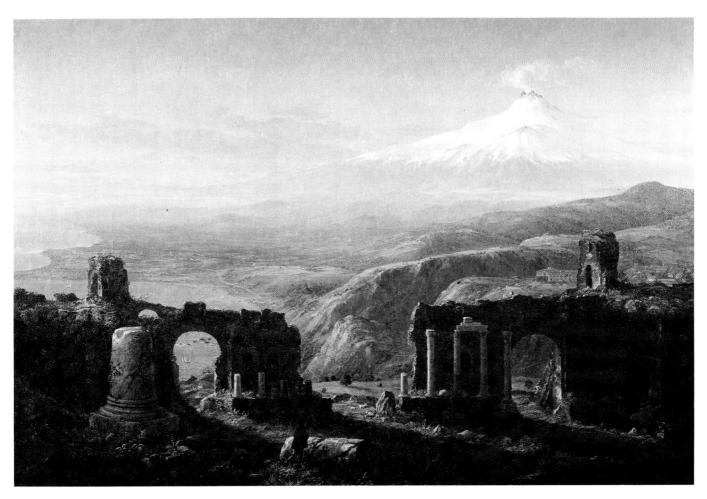

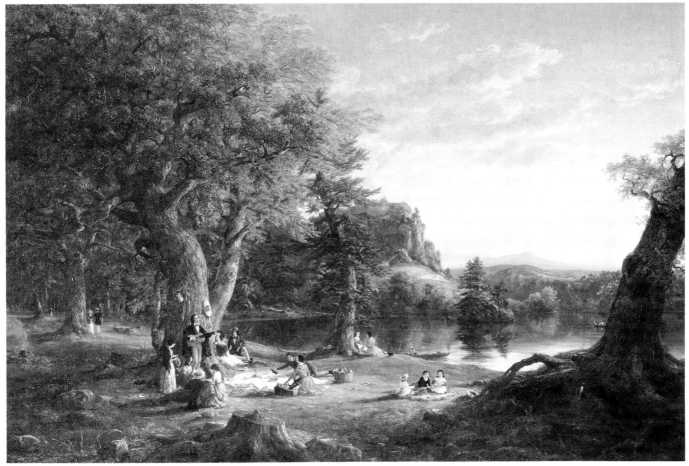

Plate 29

SCHROON LAKE
ca. 1846. Oil on canvas,
37½″ x 31″ (95 x 79 cm).
Adirondack Museum,
Blue Lake, New York.

Schroon Lake is one of Cole's most complex pictorial compositions. Within a *trompe l'oeil* circular frame he painted a landscape that includes hillocks, mountains, a land spit, a lake, and a waterfall, as well as buildings and other indications of human presence. Broad horizontal and diagonal rhythms provide a sense of energy, belying the fact that the viewer is actually placed at a great distance from the closest portion of land. It is as if Cole were making an illustration of a passage in a work by Richard Payne Knight, one of the arbiters of Picturesque taste. Knight wanted artists to portray "romantic" scenery in which "every object is wild, abrupt, and fantastic;—in which endless intricacies discover, at every turn, something new and unexpected; so that we are at once amused and surprised, and curiosity is constantly gratified, but never satiated."[90] Cole was particularly attracted to the several quiet lakes of New York State and New England. He found in their transparent repose both a calmness and a sublimity that reflect the range of his responses to their coves, shorelines, surrounding mountains, unknown depths, and shimmering surfaces. He wrote the following poem about Sylvan Lake in the Catskills:

Around the mountains forest-crowned and
    green,
    Majestic rise,
Above, like love's triumphal arch, are seen
    The quiet skies.

How spread the waters like a crystal sea
    When breezes die,
And in their lucent depths cloud, hill and tree
    Reflected lie!

Wouldst thou know peace that lore can ne'er
    reveal?
    Bend o'er the tide,

And to thy heart its tranquil clearness feel
    Serenity glide.[91]

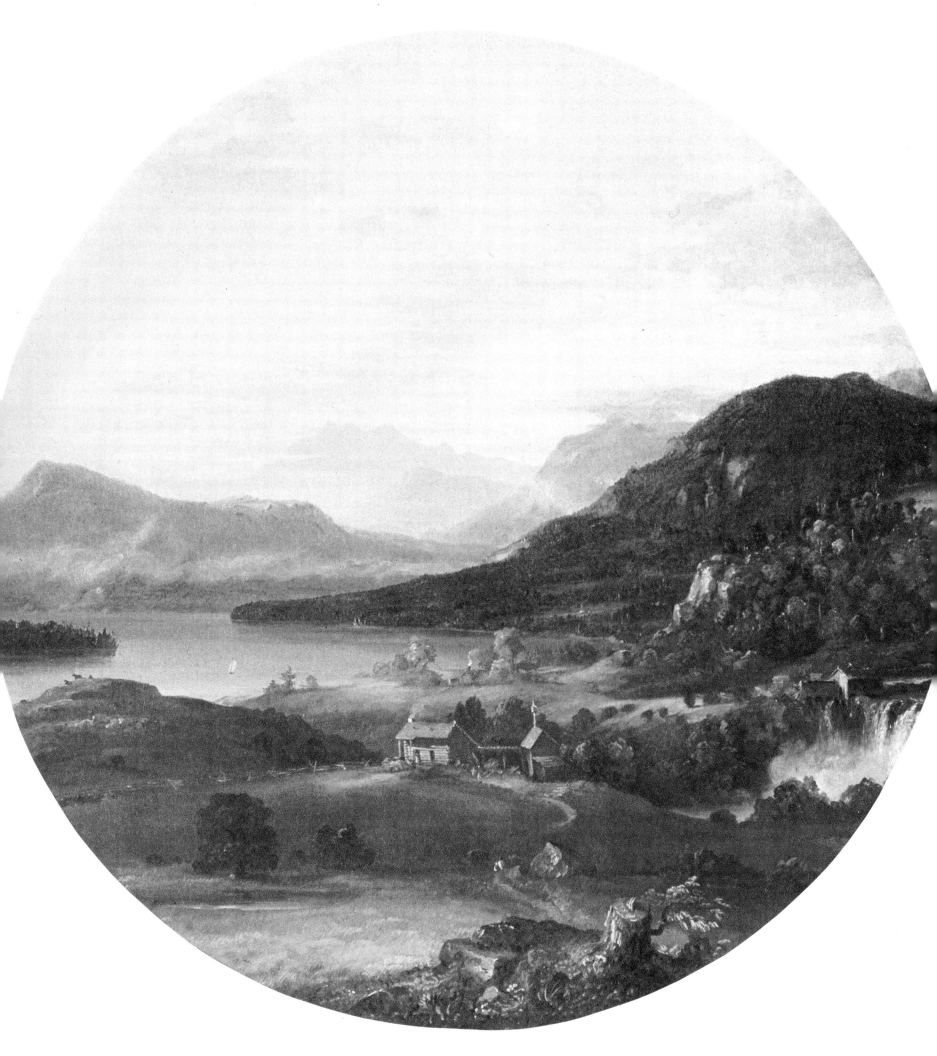

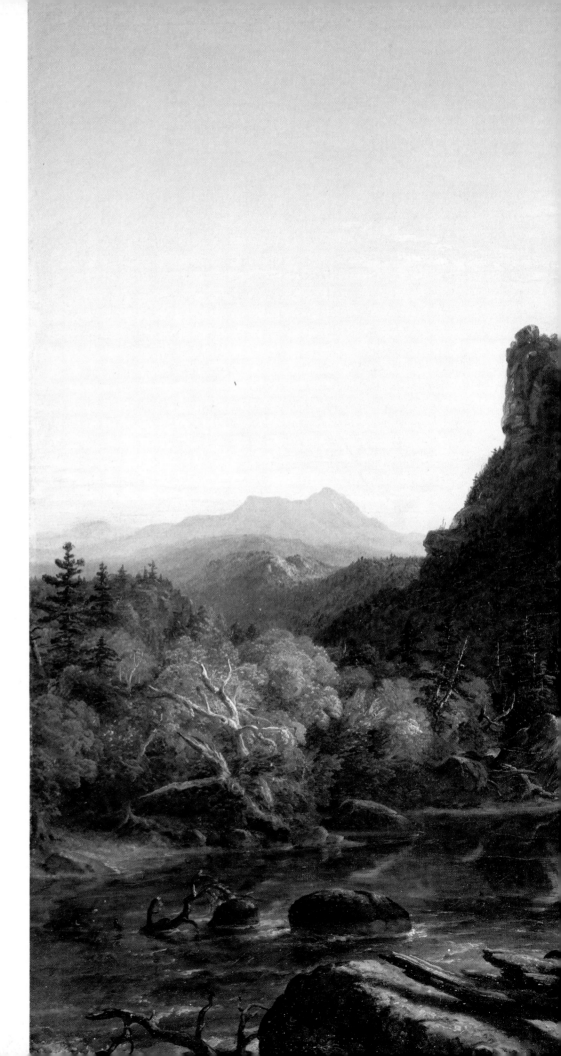

Plate 30

THE MOUNTAIN FORD
1846. Oil on canvas,
28½″ x 40″ (72 x 102 cm).
The Metropolitan Museum of Art, New York.
Bequest of Maria DeWitt Jesup
from the collection of her husband
Morris K. Jesup, 1915.

One of Cole's most handsome landscapes, *The Mountain Ford* is also one of his most mysterious. A costumed rider on a white horse fords a stream in the wilderness. Although the landscape resembles *The Notch of the White Mountains* (Plate 21), and the vertical abutment on the mountain's left flank recalls a similar shape in *The Last of the Mohicans* (Plate 8), it does not appear to be an ordinary view of charming scenery somewhere in the Adirondacks or the White Mountains, nor does the rider appear to be an ordinary woodsman or wanderer. The gait and color of the horse, the clothing and hat of the horseman, and the sense of enchantment that envelops the painting suggest that Cole was illustrating a story or legend. Sir Walter Scott's writings are a possible source, although the figure is not in medieval dress or kilts, the type of garb worn by several Scott characters.

Compositionally, the right side of *The Mountain Ford* is heavily weighted with trees, one of whose branches continues the right profile of the mountain virtually to the corner of the canvas. Since the painting opens to the left, it may have been planned as one of a pair, its mate intended to be hung at its left. If this were the case, the companion picture would have had to have been planned with a correspondingly large tree or other form at its extreme left side to close the tableau. Or, perhaps, a third and centrally placed painting might have been planned to tie together the compositional strands from the left and the right and to indicate more specifically the quest or destination of the horseman. Such compositional relationships occur in *The Departure* and its companion, *The Return* (Figure 7), as well as in *The Course of Empire* (Plates 14 and 15).

74

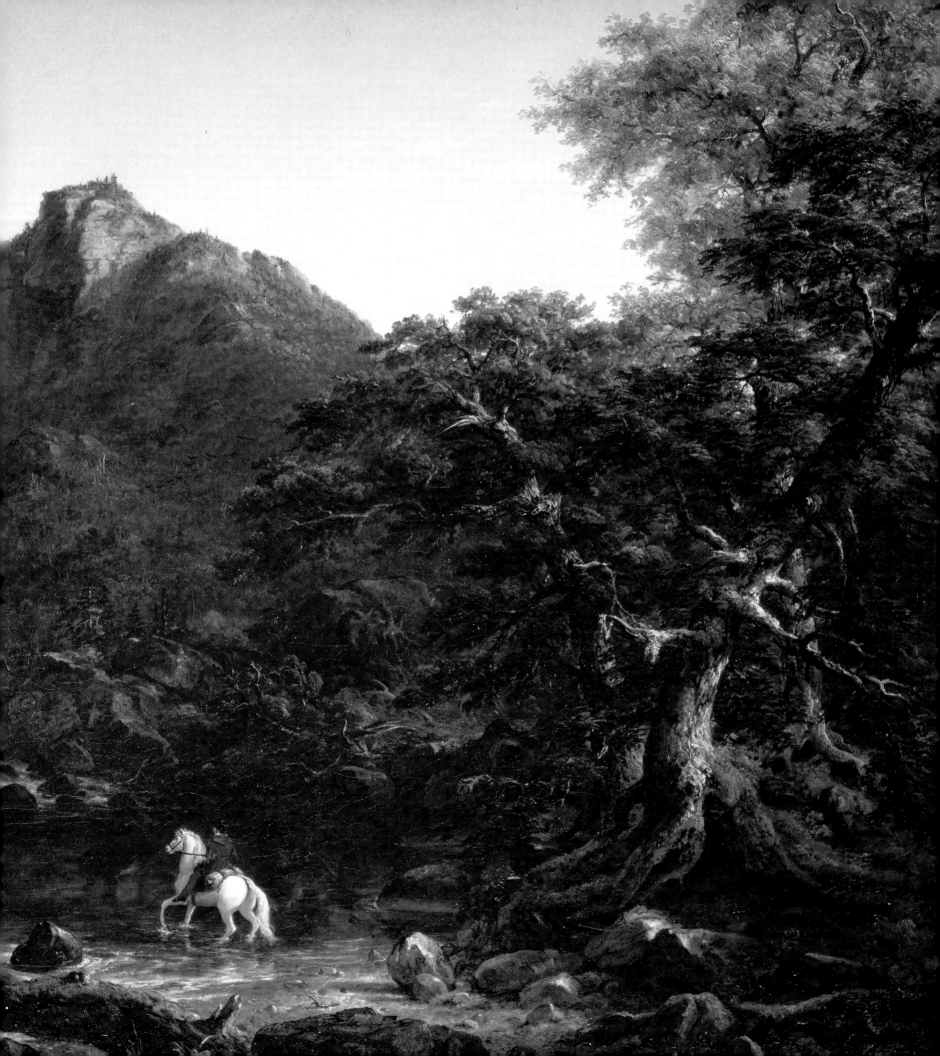

Plate 31

GENESEE SCENERY
(MOUNTAIN LANDSCAPE
WITH WATERFALL)
1847. Oil on canvas,
51" x 39½" (130 x 100 cm).
Museum of Art,
Rhode Island School of Design,
Providence.

Genesee Scenery is probably the best example of Cole's "salon" style of the 1840s. As in his earliest paintings, crossed diagonals dominate the compositional scheme, but the differences are more important than the similarities. The viewer is not thrust into the landscape but is kept at a distance from it. Forms are small in scale, and the waterfall is placed too far away for its physical presence to be "felt." The force of its impact is softened by a strategically placed bush and bent tree. The bridge over the falls and the dwelling on the overlook also suggest the new mood of Cole's landscapes. The wilderness is tamed, and the waterfall is to be savored as a view. This is a landscape to look upon rather than to be in.

Perhaps Cole's conversion to Episcopalianism in 1842 caused him to find less religious feeling in nature than in the Bible. He might still find solace in his walks in the woods, but not the earlier profound sense of religious revelation. The landscape is, instead, an amiable one, a celebration of beautiful scenery rather than an act of communion. In this regard, Cole's work of this decade accurately reflects the encroachment of American civilization onto wilderness areas. Paintings of wilderness areas done after this time were, in effect, retrospective—commemorations of what had been rather than of what was. To his credit, Cole understood this, if his paintings are any indication, better than all other landscape painters.

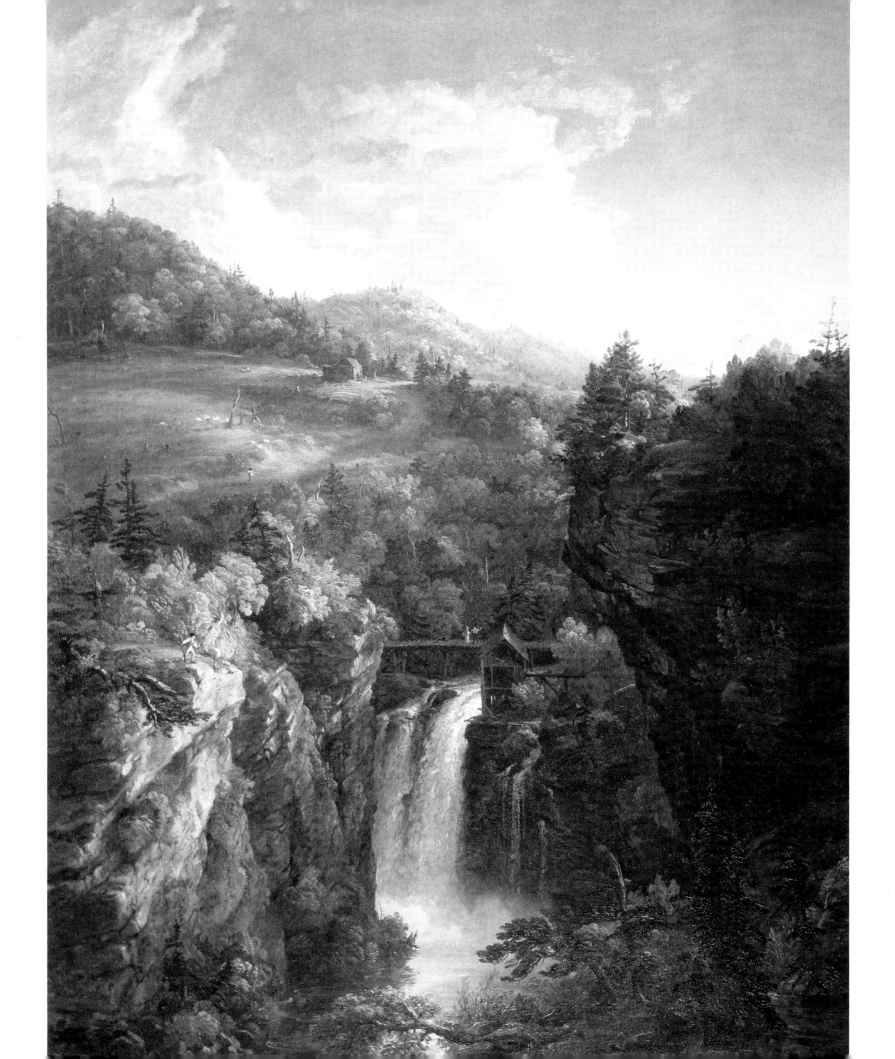

Plate 32

HOME IN THE WOODS
1847. Oil on canvas,
44" x 66" (112 x 168 cm).
Reynolda House,
Winston-Salem, North Carolina.

In *Home in the Woods*, Cole returned to a theme he had explored in the past—the frontier settlement or the cabin in the woods. In works with this theme the landscape is elevated above the raw, savage state but has not yet arrived at the pastoral stage. Here the father is returning with his catch to his happy family. The well-made cabin, the laundry drying in the sun, the clean children, and the fond exchange of greetings indicate that this area of the wilderness has been domesticated. Yet only the children have leisure time to enjoy nature. Their parents still have to work to survive, the father as a hunter rather than a farmer. Perhaps the cleared land behind the cabin will soon become a field, but existence still appears precarious. Since nature is seen in a smiling aspect, however, there is no doubt about the outcome. This is a rare instance when Cole conferred dignity upon the hardworking yeomen who were bringing civilization to the wilds. (The farmer never received his just deserts at the hands of American painters.) In contrast to Italian peasants, whom Cole loathed, these American pioneers are energetically building the nation's bright future.

In an otherwise completely secular painting, a wooden cross marks the intersection of two broad diagonals that proceed in interrupted fashion along edges of trees, the cabins, and darkened clumps of foliage. Perhaps the cross reflects Cole's thoughts which he added to his "Essay on American Scenery" when it was republished in 1841. In the later version he said that rural nature provides intellectual enjoyment, allows increased responses to works of genius, keener perceptions of the beauty of our existence, and "a more profound reverence for the Creator of all things."[92] Finally, in the catalog of the American Art Union, which commissioned the painting, the following lines were appended to the entry:

> And minds have there been nurtured, whose control
> Is felt even in their nation's destiny;
> Men who swayed senates with a statesman's soul
> And looked on armies with a leader's eye.[93]

Cole, who was not fond of Jacksonian politics, might have been making a pointed reference to Whig politician William Henry Harrison, whose victorious presidential campaign of 1840 was based on his presumed log-cabin origins.

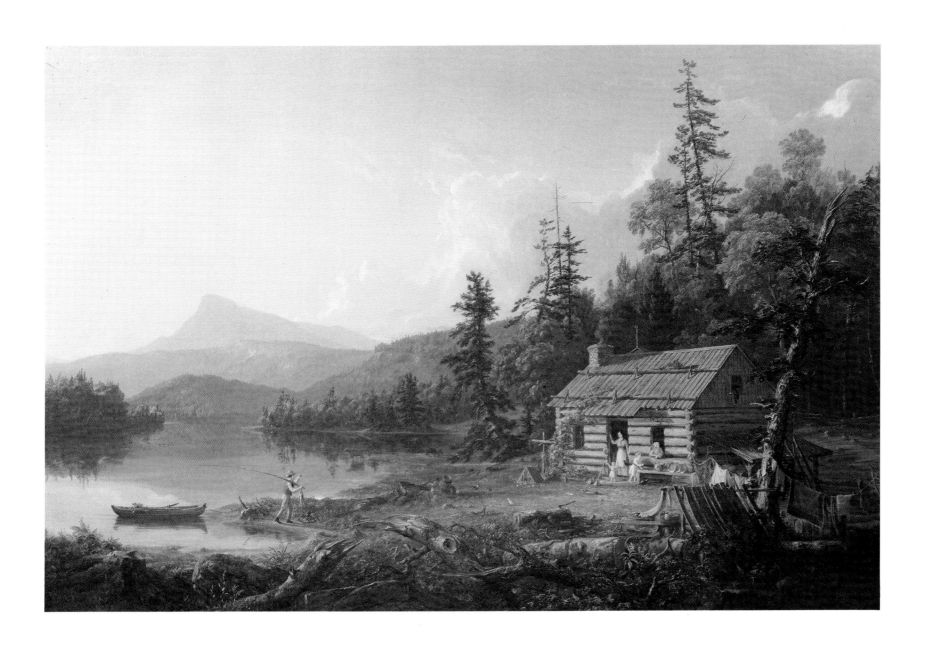

1. From "The Wild," New York State Library, photostat in the New-York Historical Society.

2. From Cole's unpublished essays, "Influence of the Plastic Arts" (1840) and "Notes on Art" (1829), cited respectively in Kenneth James LaBudde, "The Mind of Thomas Cole" (Ph.D. diss., University of Minnesota, 1954), p. 161; and John C. Riordan, "Thomas Cole: A Case Study of the Painter-Poet Theory of Art in American Painting from 1825 to 1859" (Ph.D. diss., Syracuse University, 1970), p. 274.

3. William Charvat, *The Origins of American Critical Thought, 1810–1835* (Philadelphia: University of Pennsylvania Press, 1936), *passim.*

4. Perry Miller, "The Romantic Dilemma in American Nationalism and the Concept of Nature," *Harvard Theological Review* 48 (October 1955): 239–53.

5. John Haviland, *The Builder's Assistant*, 3 vols. (Philadelphia, 1818, 1819, 1821), 3:37.

6. See especially Donald A. Ringe, *The Pictorial Mode: Space and Time in the Art of Bryant, Irving and Cooper* (Lexington: University Press of Kentucky, 1971), and Blake Nevius, *Cooper's Landscapes* (Berkeley: University of California Press, 1976).

7. The entire correspondence is included in the Baltimore Museum of Art, *Annual II: Studies on Thomas Cole, an American Romanticist* (Baltimore, 1967), pp. 43–81.

8. Ibid., p. 79.

9. Louis L. Noble, *The Life of Thomas Cole*, ed. Elliot S. Vessell (Cambridge: Harvard University Press, 1964), p. 185.

10. William Palmer Hudson, "Archibald Alison and William Cullen Bryant," *American Literature* 12 (March 1940): 60.

11. The edition of Alison's *Essays* used in this study was published in New York in 1830 by Carvill. See pp. 21–22, 79–80.

12. Ibid., p. 18.

13. Jerome Stolnitz, "Of the Origins of 'Aesthetic Distinterestedness,'" in *Aesthetics: A Critical Anthology*, ed. George Dickie and R. J. Sclafani (New York: St. Martin's Press, 1977), p. 617.

14. Alison, *Essays*, pp. 412, 414–15.

15. See, for example, Robert Streeter, "Associ-ation Psychology and Literary Nationalism in the *North American Review*, 1815–1825," *American Literature* 17 (1945): 243–54; Donald A. Ringe, "Kindred Spirits: Bryant and Cole," *American Quarterly*, Fall 1954, pp. 233–44; and Ralph N. Miller, "Thomas Cole and Alison's *Essays on Taste*," *New York History* 37 (July 1956); 281–99.

16. From the *North American Review*, December 1818, cited in Miller, *Nature's Nation* (Cambridge, Mass.: Harvard University Press, 1967), p. 20.

17. Thaddeus Mason Harris, *Journal of a Tour into the Territory Northwest of the Allegheny Mountains* (1805), cited in both Ringe, *The Pictorial Mode*, p. 22; and Roderick Nash, *Wilderness and the American Mind*, rev. ed. (New Haven: Yale University Press, 1973), p. 58.

18. From the poem "Etna," photostat in the New-York Historical Society.

19. Russel Blaine Nye, *Society and Culture in America, 1830–1860* (New York: Harper & Row, 1974), p. 91.

20. Nevius, *Cooper's Landscapes*, p. 55; and Stanley T. Williams, "Cosmopolitanism in American Literature Before 1880," in *The American Writer and the European Tradition*, ed. Margaret Denny and William H. Gilmer (New York: McGraw-Hill, 1964), pp. 45–62.

21. Noble, *Life*, p. 219.

22. Ibid., p. 148.

23. Darrell Garwood, *Artist in Iowa: A Life of Grant Wood* (New York: Norton, 1944), p. 153.

24. Thomas Cole, "Essay on American Scenery," *The American Monthly Magazine*, N.S. 1 (January 1836): 1–12, reproduced in John W. McCoubrey, ed., *American Art, 1700–1960* (Englewood Cliffs, N.J.: Prentice-Hall, 1965), pp. 108–9.

25. Letters, Cole to Robert Gilmor, Jr., April 29, 1829, and January 29, 1832, *Annual II*, pp. 67 and 74; and Noble, *Life*, p. 249.

26. Ellwood C. Parry III, "Thomas Cole's 'The Course of Empire': A Study in Serial Imagery" (Ph.D. diss., Yale University, 1970), *passim.*

27. Nevius, *Cooper's Landscapes*, pp. 27–28; and from Cole's Notebooks and Sketchbooks, 1825–1847, in the Detroit Institute of Arts, reproduced on microfilm, Archives of American Art, roll D39, frame 150.

28. Marvin Meyers, *The Jacksonian Persuasion* (Palo Alto, Calif.: Stanford University Press, 1957), p. 102.

29. Noble, *Life*, p. 140; and Kenneth J. LaBudde, "The Rural Earth: Sylvan Bliss," *American Quarterly* 10 (Summer 1958): 144.

30. James Fenimore Cooper, *The Pathfinder* (New York: New American Library, 1961; originally published in 1840), p. 25.

31. Alf Evers, *The Catskills: From Wilderness to Woodstock* (Garden City, N.Y.: Doubleday, 1972), pp. 351, 375.

32. From Sketchbook 3, Detroit Institute of Arts, 39.560, in typescript in the New-York Historical Society.

33. Fred Somkin, *Unquiet Eagle: Memory and Desire in the Idea of American Freedom, 1815–1860* (Ithaca, N.Y.: Cornell University Press, 1967), pp. 18, 49. See also Nye, *Society and Culture*, p. 36.

34. Curtis Dahl, "The American School of Catastrophe," *American Quarterly* 11 (Fall 1959): 380–90; and Somkin, *Unquiet Eagle*, pp. 48–49.

35. From Cole's Journal for August 21, 1835, cited in LaBudde, "Mind of Thomas Cole," pp. 147–48.

36. Letter, Gilmor to Cole, December 13, 1826, *Annual II*, p. 45.

37. John F. Kasson, *Civilizing the Machine: Technology and Republican Values in America, 1776–1900* (New York: Penguin Books, 1977), p. 63.

38. Original in New York State Library, photostat in New-York Historical Society.

39. Sherman Paul, *Emerson's Angle of Vision* (Cambridge, Mass.: Harvard University Press, 1952), p. 37.

40. Eugene L. Huddleston, "Topographical Poetry in the Early National Period," *American Literature* 38 (November 1966); 312–13.

41. Timothy Dwight, *Travels in New England and New York (1796–1815)*, 4 vols. (New Haven, 1821–22), 4:177, cited in Evers, *Catskills*, p. 227.

42. Ibid., pp. 362–63.

43. Noble, *Life*, pp. 41–42.

44. Jessie V. V. Vedder, *Official History of Greene County* (New York: Greene County Board of

Supervisors, 1927), pp. 96, 99–100. Photographs of both falls are in Ernest Ingersoll, *Illustrated Guide to the Hudson River and Catskill Mountains* (New York: Rand McNally, 1909), facing pp. 140, 156.

45. Original in New York State Library, photostat in New-York Historical Society.

46. Letter, Gilmor to Cole, December 13, 1826; and Letter, Cole to Gilmor, December 25, 1826, *Annual II*, pp. 44–47.

47. William Gilpin, *Remarks on Forest Scenery, and Other Woodland Views*, 2 vols., 3d ed. (London, 1808), 2:250–51, cited in Earl A. Powell III, "Thomas Cole and the American Landscape Tradition: The Picturesque," *Arts Magazine* 52 (March 1978): 115.

48. For "The Bewilderment," original in New York State Library, copy in New-York Historical Society; for "Before Sunrise," original in Detroit Institute of Arts, microfilm in Archives of American Art, roll D6, frame 31; for "Morning," original in Detroit Institute of Arts, microfilm in Archives of American Art, roll D6, frame 16; description of sunrise in Noble, *Life*, p. 39.

49. Noble, *Life*, pp. 41, 67; and McCoubrey, ed., *American Art*, p. 106.

50. James T. Callow, *Kindred Spirits: Knickerbocker Writers and American Artists, 1807–1855* (Chapel Hill: University of North Carolina Press, 1967), pp. 132–33.

51. William Cullen Bryant, *A Funeral Oration Occasioned by the Death of Thomas Cole* (New York: Appleton, 1848), p. 14.

52. Letter, Cole to Gilmor, May 21, 1828, *Annual II*, p. 58.

53. Parry, "Thomas Cole's 'Course of Empire,' " pp. 18–19.

54. McCoubrey, ed., *American Art*, pp. 99–100.

55. Howard S. Merritt, "A Wild Scene, Genesis of a Painting," *Annual II*, pp. 7–40; and Parry, "Thomas Cole's 'Course of Empire,' " chapter 2.

56. Letter, Cole to Gilmor, January 29, 1832, *Annual II*, p. 72.

57. From Cole's Journal for August 24, 1831, cited in Riordan, "Thomas Cole," pp. 70–71.

58. Letter, Cole to Gilmor, January 29, 1832, *Annual II*, p. 74.

59. Charvat, *Origins*, p. 70.

60. Parry, "Thomas Cole's 'Course of Empire,' " p. 21.

61. Cited in *Selected Paintings and Sculpture from the Yale University Art Gallery* (New Haven: Yale University Press, 1972), entry 59.

62. Parry, "Thomas Cole's 'Course of Empire,' " p. 21.

63. E. Anna Lewis, "Art and Artists of America: Thomas Cole, N.A.," *Graham's Magazine* 46 (1855): 333.

64. Cited in Parker Lesley, "Thomas Cole and the Romantic Sensibility," *Art Quarterly* 5 (1942): 211.

65. Letter, Cole to Luman Reed, September 18, 1833, cited in Parry, "Thomas Cole's 'Course of Empire,' " pp. 143–45.

66. Alan Wallach, "Cole, Byron and 'Course of Empire,' " *Art Bulletin* 50 (December 1968): 378.

67. From Cole's printed description of *The Course of Empire*, cited in Parry, "Thomas Cole's 'Course of Empire,' " p. 194.

68. Ibid., pp. 108, 112.

69. From Cole's Journal for August 21, 1835, cited in LaBudde, "Mind of Thomas Cole," pp. 147–48.

70. Parry, "Thomas Cole's 'Course of Empire,' " p. 115.

71. McCoubrey, ed., *American Art*, p. 100.

72. Original in New York State Library, photostat in New-York Historical Society.

73. Nevius, *Cooper's Landscapes*, chapters 3 and 4.

74. William Dunlap, *History of the Rise and Progress of the Arts of Design in the United States* (1834), 3 vols., ed. Alexander Wyckoff (New York, 1965), 3:154.

75. Ovid, *Metamorphoses*, trans. Rolfe Humphries (Bloomington: Indiana University Press, 1955), Book I, lines 88–111.

76. From an essay describing his trip to the White Mountains with George Platt, October 2, 1828, in Notebooks and Sketchbooks, 1825–1847, in the Detroit Institute of Arts, on microfilm in Archives of American Art, roll D39, frame 260.

77. Noble, *Life*, p. 179.

78. From his "Essay on American Scenery," in McCoubrey, ed., *American Art*, p. 103.

79. Noble, *Life*, p. 66.

80. Dahl, "American School of Catastrophe," p. 390.

81. Noble, *Life*, p. 67.

82. Alan Wallach, "The *Voyage of Life* as Popular Art," *Art Bulletin* 59 (June 1977): 239.

83. McCoubrey, ed., *American Art*, p. 108.

84. Huddleston, "Topographical Poetry," 304.

85. Noble, *Life*, p. 164; and LaBudde, "Mind of Thomas Cole," pp. 147, 143. The last citation is from Cole's Journal for August 1, 1836.

86. Cole, "The Lament of the Forest," *The Knickerbocker* 17 (June 1, 1841): 516–19.

87. Ringe, *Pictorial Mode*, p. 182.

88. Cole, "Sicilian Scenery and Antiquities," *The Knickerbocker* 23 (February 1844): 14.

89. Ibid. (March 1844): 241.

90. Richard Payne Knight, *An Analytical Inquiry into the Principles of Taste*, 4th ed. (London, 1808), p. 195, cited in Nevius, *Cooper's Landscapes*, p. 20.

91. Original in the New York State Library, photostat in New-York Historical Society.

92. Cole, "Lecture on American Scenery," *The Northern Light* 1 (May 1841): 25.

93. Cited in Barbara B. Lassiter, *Reynolda House: American Paintings* (New York: Hirschl and Adler Galleries, 1970), p. 20.

Archival Material

Most of Cole's extant writings and drawings are in the Detroit Institute of Arts and the Albany Institute of History and Art, Albany, New York. Material in the latter collection is duplicated on photostats in the New-York Historical Society, New York. The Archives of American Art has microfilms of both the Detroit and Albany collections. Additional original material is in the Museum of Fine Arts, Boston, and the Princeton University Art Museum, Princeton, New Jersey.

Writings by Thomas Cole

"Essay on American Scenery." *American Monthly Magazine*, n.s. 1 (January 1836): 1–12. Reprinted in John W. McCoubrey, ed. *American Art, 1700–1960, Sources and Documents*. Englewood Cliffs, N.J.: Prentice-Hall, 1965.

"Lecture on American Scenery." *The Northern Light* 1 (May 1841): 25–26.

"Sicilian Scenery and Antiquities." *Knickerbocker Magazine* 23 (February 1844): 103–13, and (March 1844): 236–44.

Books and Catalogs

Baltimore Museum of Art. *Annual II. Studies on Thomas Cole, an American Romanticist*. Baltimore, 1967.

Dunlap, William. *History of the Rise and Progress of the Arts of Design in the United States*. 2 vols. New York, 1834. Reissued with additions by F. W. Bayley and C. E. Goodspeed. 3 vols. Boston, 1918. Revised, enlarged ed. by Alexander Wykoff. Preface by William Campbell. 3 vols. New York: Blom, 1965.

Kennedy Galleries, New York City. *An Exhibition of Paintings by Thomas Cole, N.A., from the Artist's Studio, Catskill, New York*. 1964.

Merrit, Howard S. *Thomas Cole*. Rochester Memorial Art Gallery of the University of Rochester, 1969.

Nathan, W. L. "Thomas Cole and the Romantic Landscape." In *Romanticism in America*, edited by George Boas. Baltimore: Johns Hopkins Press, 1940.

Noble, Louis L. *The Course of Empire, Voyage of Life and Other Pictures of Thomas Cole, N.A.* (1853). Reissued with an introduction by Elliot S. Vessell as *The Life and Works of Thomas Cole*. Cambridge, Mass.: Harvard University Press, 1964.

Seaver, Esther I. *Thomas Cole, One Hundred Years Later*. Hartford: Wadsworth Atheneum, 1948.

Tymn, Marshall, ed. *Thomas Cole's Poetry*. York, Pa.: Liberty Cap Books, 1972.

Articles

Clarke, John R. "An Italian Landscape by Thomas Cole." *Arts Magazine* 54 (January 1980): 116–20.

Dwight, Edward H., and Boyle, Richard J. "Rediscovery: Thomas Cole's 'Voyage of Life.'" *Art in America* 55 (May-June 1967): 60–63.

Hale, Edward E. "The Early Art of Thomas Cole." *Art in America* 4 (1916): 22–40.

LaBudde, Kenneth J. "The Rural Earth: Sylvan Bliss." *American Quarterly* 10 (1958): 142–53.

Lesley, E. Parker. "Some Clues to Thomas Cole." *Magazine of Art* 42 (February 1949): 42–48.

———. "Thomas Cole and the Romantic Sensibility." *Art Quarterly* 5 (Summer 1942): 198–221.

Miller, Ralph N. "Thomas Cole and Alison's *Essays on Taste*." *New York History* 37 (1956): 281–99.

Moore, James C. "Thomas Cole's *The Cross and the World*: Recent Findings." *The American Art Journal* 5 (1973): 50–60.

Novak, Barbara. "Thomas Cole and Robert Gilmor." *Art Quarterly* 25 (1962): 41–53.

Parry, Ellwood C., III. "Gothic Elegies for an American Audience: Thomas Cole's Repackaging of Imported Ideas." *The American Art Journal* 8 (November 1976): 26–46.

———. "Thomas Cole and the Problem of Figure Painting." *The American Art Journal* 4 (Spring 1972): 77–86.

———. "Thomas Cole's Imagination at Work in *The Architect's Dream*." *The American Art Journal* 12 (Winter 1980): 41–59.

Powell, Earl A., III. "Thomas Cole and the American Landscape Tradition: Associationism." *Arts Magazine* 52 (April 1978): 113–17.

———. "Thomas Cole and the American Landscape Tradition: The Naturalist Controversy." *Arts Magazine* 52 (February 1978): 114–23.

———. "Thomas Cole and the American Landscape Tradition: The Picturesque." *Arts Magazine* 52 (March 1978): 110–17.

Ringe, Donald A. "James Fenimore Cooper and Thomas Cole: An Analogous Technique." *American Literature* 30 (1958): 26–36.

———. "Kindred Spirits: Bryant and Cole." *American Quarterly* 6 (1954): 233–44.

———. "Painting as Poem in the Hudson River Aesthetic." *American Quarterly* 12 (1960): 71–83.

Sanford, Charles L. "The Concept of the Sublime in the Works of Thomas Cole and William Cullen Bryant." *American Literature* 28 (1956–57): 434–48.

Schmitt, Evelyn L. "Two American Romantics—Thomas Cole and William Cullen Bryant." *Art in America* 41 (Spring 1953): 61–68.

Wallach, Alan. "Cole, Byron and 'Course of Empire.'" *Art Bulletin* 50 (December 1968): 375–79.

———. "Thomas Cole: British Esthetics and American Scenery." *Artforum* 8 (October 1969): 46–49.

———. The 'Voyage of Life' as Popular Art." *Art Bulletin* 59 (June 1977): 234–41.

Dissertations

LaBudde, Kenneth J. "The Mind of Thomas Cole." Ph.D. dissertation, University of Minnesota, 1954.

Novak, Barbara. "Cole and Durand: Criticism and Patronage (A Study of American Taste in Landscape, 1825–1865)." Ph.D. dissertation, Radcliffe College, 1957.

Parry, Ellwood C., III. "Thomas Cole's 'The Course of Empire': A Study in Serial Imagery." Ph.D. dissertation, Yale University, 1970.

Riordan, John. "Thomas Cole: A Case Study of the Painter-Poet Theory of Art in American Painting from 1825 to 1850." Ph.D. dissertation, Syracuse University, 1970.

Wallach, Alan. "The Ideal American Artist and the Dissenting Tradition: A Study of Thomas Cole's Popular Reputation." Ph.D. dissertation, Columbia University, 1973.

Edited by Betty Vera
Designed by Bob Fillie
Graphic Production by Ellen Greene
Text set in 10-point Baskerville